DISCOVER AMERICA

DISCOVER AMERICA
The Smithsonian Book of the National Parks

Charles E. Little
Photographs by David Muench

Smithsonian Books, Washington, D.C.

The Smithsonian Institution

Secretary I. Michael Heyman

Acting Director, Smithsonian Institution Press Daniel Goodwin

Smithsonian Books

Editor-in-Chief Patricia Gallagher

Senior Editor Alexis Doster III

Editors Amy Donovan, Joe Goodwin

Associate Editors Bryan D. Kennedy, Sonia Reece

Assistant Editor Robert Lockhart

Copy Editor Elizabeth Dahlslien Gelfeld

Senior Picture Editor Frances C. Rowsell

Picture Editors Carrie E. Bruns, R. Jenny Takacs

Associate Picture Editor Paula Dailey

Picture Researcher Lynn A. Sahaydak

Production Editor Patricia Upchurch

Business Manager Stephen J. Bergstrom

Marketing Manager Susan E. Romatowski

©1995 Smithsonian Institution

Manufactured in the United States of America

First Edition

02 01 00 99 98 97 96 95

5 4 3 2 1

Distributed to the trade by Smithsonian Institution Press

Library of Congress Cataloging-in-Publication Data

Little, Charles E.
    Discover America: the Smithsonian book of the national parks/by Charles E. Little: photographs by David Muench.
      p. cm.
    Includes index.
    ISBN 0-89599-050-4
    1. National parks and reserves—United States—History.
2. National parks and reserves—United States—Guidebooks.
3. National parks and reserves—United States—Pictorial works.
I. Smithsonian Institution. II. Title.
E160.L57 1995
973—dc20   95-33596
                             CIP

From the national parks: (page 1) a winter sunrise in Grand Teton National Park, Wyoming; (page 2–3) sunset over Bearfence Mountain, Shenandoah National Park, Virginia; and above, cannons and the New York monument, Antietam National Battlefield, Maryland.

CONTENTS

FOREWORD

T. S. ELIOT ONCE REMARKED THAT HISTORY HAS MANY CUNNING CORRIDORS, and the genesis of the book you are about to read illustrates this. The basic idea for it was conceived when photographer David Muench and I shared an idea early in the 1980s. Was there a place for yet another book on national parks, one that would offer the main themes of American history—starting from the Bering Strait 20,000 years or so ago—solely through carefully selected National Park Service areas? We explored the idea intensively and consulted with colleagues and friends in the service and in the field of American history. They liked our conception, and we agreed to see if we could get a publisher.

It wasn't until we discussed the project with Smithsonian Books that we found a sympathetic response. Further, they explored the idea that the book should link human history with natural history. I considered this to be a wise decision, for I had long thought that we must learn to relate human history to our environment. At that point, I was pleased to give up the role of prospective author and to serve as editorial consultant, especially since I would then have more time to deal with my voluminous archives in the field of historic preservation.

Smithsonian Books turned to Charles E. Little, an author they knew well, and asked him for an outline. I thought the outline brilliantly presented both sides of the ecosystem that is the United States of America, offering the possibility of a new kind of book about the national parks. I realized that he recognized that the history of our country begins and ends with infinity, a progression from creation to civilization.

As a result, I thought how pleased my longtime friend, the late Horace Marden Albright, second director of the park service, would have been, for it was he who first envisioned the intertwining of human history and natural history through the national park system. It was a vision that was enhanced by the man Albright had hired as the service's first chief historian, Verne E. Chatelain, who in April 1933 made an astonishing prediction: "The sum total of the sites which we select should make it possible to tell a more or less complete story about American history." A wise man, he also knew that history embraces both humanity and nature, and he began to share his point of view with the old-time superintendents and rangers west of the Mississippi.

During the five years that Chatelain remained with the service, he advanced the cause of historic preservation in many ways, and defined its limits. Working closely with Horace Albright in all matters, he dealt effectively with the complex negotiations for the legislation that brought into being on

African-American educator Booker T. Washington was born a slave in this

Franklin County, Virginia, cabin (left) in 1856. It is now a National Monument.

7

Horace Albright, pictured in 1919, the year he became superintendent of Yellowstone. Ten years later, Albright succeeded Stephen Mather as director of the National Park Service.

March 2, 1933, the system's first national historical park, at Morristown, New Jersey. As the late Charles B. Hosmer, Jr., has pointed out in his great works on the history of historic preservation, Chatelain was a principal in framing one of the seminal pieces of legislation in the field, the Historic Sites Act of 1935. Chatelain went on to outline what a truly national preservation program should be, and broadened the concept by saying that "no park or monument should be entirely free of historical activities," causing a shudder to go through the ranger forces in the Western states. Unmoved, his vision led him to anticipate that the park service would eventually have to deal with the Lewis and Clark exploration story. He preached research and professionalism, and brought together a group of young historians doing graduate work at the University of Minnesota who would become the future leaders in the field. He urged Americans to travel, because, said he, it was the "way that no amount of reading and study of written records can make possible." (And this is a credo exemplified by Charles Little's words in the pages ahead.) To sum up, as Charles Hosmer noted, Albright and Chatelain "complemented each other in their optimism and ambition." And they led the way.

Now, with the national park system so newly defined, let me carry the story forward at a swifter pace. The New Deal, through its many programs, became the primary pre-World War II force in expanding the system. One program that Horace Albright intuitively recognized to be significant was the setting up of the Civilian Conservation Corps. Within months in the spring of 1933, he put into national and state parks hundreds of units, all working on historical and environmental projects. Equally important was his success in getting President Franklin Delano Roosevelt to authorize an executive order that brought all battlefields, monuments, and cemeteries administered by the War Department and Forest Service into the Department of the Interior, a story that author Charles Little tells in more detail in his first chapter.

World War II brought a lull in park service activities, and director Newton B. Drury had to stand firm to keep the national parks from being raided by business and by other federal agencies. Some service personnel served in the war; when it ended, they were happy to be back once again in their old jobs. But it would be an arduous climb into the mid-'50s before there was support for a well-conceived, 10-year program that was called Mission 66 to mark its termination date. It had support, but it's a strange truth that some Presidents and some Congresses were loathe to give adequate support to the national park system even as its attendance rose—and rose. In the chapters that follow, readers will discover that the struggle for adequate support is still going on.

I think I should offer a clue as to what led David Muench and me to think seriously about a book called "History on the Land." A colleague and friend, the late Melvin Weig, under whom I worked at Morristown, New Jersey, in 1937, put together, experimentally, a slide-and-sound lecture for orientation. (This was not a new technique, for I have a record of an employee of the New York State Historical Association, when its headquarters was in Saratoga in 1911, using the same technique.) I watched and learned. It was approved by our superintendent, Elbert Cox, the second historian employed by the service when it expanded its operations in the early 1930s. In the years

The Virgin River flows through a narrow canyon at the foot of steep cliffs in Zion National Park, Utah.

that followed, Melvin Weig developed a slide-and-sound presentation covering many of the historical parks throughout the country; he called it "History on the Land," and gave me a copy. This, I feel, is what made me think of a possible book bearing that title. As you will see shortly, that has become the title of the first chapter of this book. And now you know the whole story of how this book came to be.

I revel in all this because it is the fulfillment of the dream I shared with David Muench more than 10 years ago. David had already roamed through every state in our union for more than 30 years, waiting patiently in the right place at the right time to take yet another photograph that held a mirror to the past, linking nature and history. He presented many that might be called the "grand views," those that evoked awe in the first explorers, pioneers, and settlers. They were interpretations, carefully composed in order to help others see or remember. There are many memory-laden scenes in our parks, and David's photographs will still be there when memory fades.

This book, then, not only celebrates Americans' love of their land, but, in "Study Out the Land," the author gives practical and clear advice about

Foreword

The Green River cuts through Dinosaur National Monument, on the Utah-Colorado border. The sands and rocks of this ancient river hold a time capsule from the age of dinosaurs in the form of abundant fossil bone deposits.

your future travels. He comments rationally, as well, on the problems still facing the National Park Service and on what you can do to help preserve this unique system of parks that defines the American heritage. So renew your wonder through Charles Little's and David Muench's collaboration and then join the hosts of the curious by visiting your parks and viewing them intelligently. And when you go, remember that tersest of thought-provoking couplets, "No roots, no fruits."

Addendum: In the wake of having written the foregoing, a happy thought came to my wife and me. (Like George Bernard Shaw, we make a habit of thinking twice a week.) We had planned to head south this spring to Baton Rouge for a reunion of my wife's family, and it occurred to us that we could follow Charles Little's advice and drive at a leisurely pace from Nashville, Tennessee, on the park service's Natchez Trace Parkway, more than 400 miles of constantly changing territory that offers everything: a chance to walk or

even drive on parts of the old trace, farms, mines, Indian mounds, nature trails, a Chickasaw village, beaver dams, a Civil War battlefield, a restored historic house (Mount Locust), and even a bluff with a deposit of loess (topsoil) blown here during the Ice Age. I will be looking particularly for the old trace I drove on many years ago, for it was there that I was startled when a flock of wild turkeys crossed the route in front of me and, again, a few hundred yards farther along, when half a dozen deer did the same. I broke into laughter, for I knew that I was going to accuse my park service friends of flushing that flock and those deer out of the woods just for the benefit of visitors. Charles Little is right: service personnel are wonderful people.

So have fun, escape into the past. But remember the adjuration of Danish philosopher Soren Kierkegaard: "Life can only be understood backward, but it must be lived forward." Enjoy your forays into the past and the future, and then Clio, the goddess of history, will be pleased.

FREDERICK L. RATH, JR., Cooperstown, N. Y., 28 April 1995

Overleaf: *Panorama from Point Sublime*, by William Henry Holmes. This is one of a number of illustrations Holmes executed for Clarence Dutton's *Tertiary History of the Grand Cañon District*, which was published in 1882 to present the findings of Dutton's 1879 exploration of the Grand Canyon for the U.S. Geological Survey.

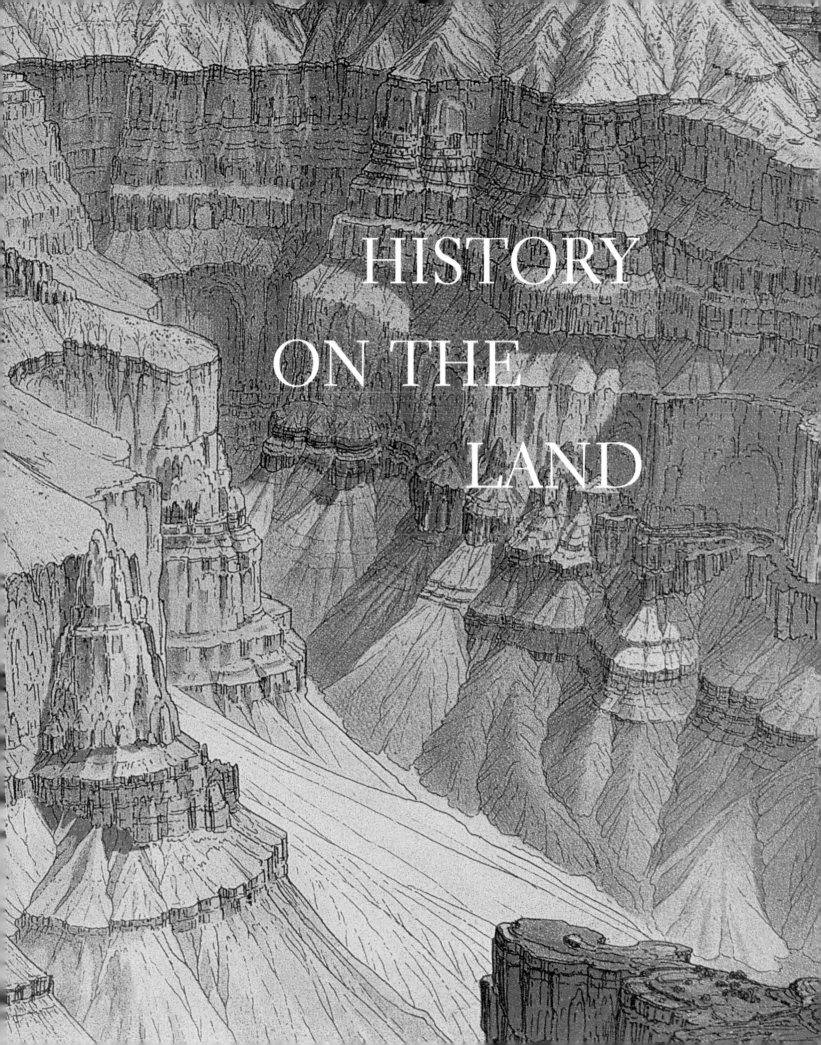

HISTORY

ON THE

LAND

Here is the test of wisdom,
Wisdom is not finally tested in schools

. . . .

Something there is in the float of the sight
of things that provokes it out of the soul.

—Walt Whitman
"Song of the Open Road"

No, the chapter title is not a misprint, for it is a singular kind of history offered here, a history on the land, as well as *of* it, a history that can be seen and felt, a history we can experience ourselves in sublime natural settings, in fossil records and archaeological ruins, and in the historical buildings, landscapes, and neighborhoods of more recent times. This is the gift of the American system of national parks. No other nation offers such a record of itself that is so accessible and, yes, so utterly moving for those wishing to examine it. The halls of this great museum of parks stretch from the edge of Siberia to the Caribbean Sea, and from the rockbound coast of New England all the way to Polynesia 10 thousand miles away. The individual units of the system number, at this writing, 368, more than any family could visit even in a half-dozen generations. And so, to read the history, visitors must be purposeful and selective, just as we—the photographer, author, editors, and the editorial consultant on the project—have been for this book. We invite you to travel with us in the ensuing pages, and then to set out on your own to explore the parks, to read the history on the land by a plan that you devise.

Our plan for the book has been largely chronological, as befits history. It begins with a description of parks that reveal geological time in the great forces that shaped the land—glaciers, volcanoes, and ineluctable erosions of wind and water that uncover the remains of creatures now extinct.

Then come the places where the "first families" settled. Declining seas opened up the broad meadowlands of Beringia, inviting the first humans to venture onto a new continent: our paleo-Indians, arriving from Siberia, whose relict homes and cities can be found in every part of the country, protected now as archaeological sites and historical parks. After many millennia passed, other immigrants arrived, this time from Europe—Spain, the Netherlands, France, England—and, under painful circumstances, from Africa and (later) Asia. All made their mark, in forts, missions, even some

Dawn breaks over an ancient bristlecone pine at Great Basin National Park, Nevada. The park is a recent (1986) creation, but the oldest known living thing on Earth—a bristlecone pine that germinated 4,950 years ago—was found here.

whole communities that are now protected and interpreted as part of the national park system.

As the European immigrants set about to explore the continent they sought to colonize, they found themselves utterly astonished by its immense wildernesses and extraordinary landforms. "Nature's Nation," Thomas Jefferson called it: the endless forests, high mountain ranges, deserts, a billion acres of grass, rivers one could hardly see across, and land animals, birds, and serpents that defied description in their size and plenitude. These features, too, are captured in a stunning array of parks.

In time (but sooner than anyone thought possible), the continent was conquered, and the frontier had all but vanished. It remained to build a nation, to "form a more perfect union," as the first words of the Preamble to the Constitution promised. And here, the park system records the effort in battlefields, in the sites of great political events, and in the celebration of leaders who dared to take the Constitution seriously—from Jefferson himself to Martin Luther King, Jr.

All of this history is written on the land in national parks, monuments, and historical areas. The nomenclature is various, with 20 titles aside from "national park" being used to describe the various units, but they are all part of our national park system.

How did such a wealth of parks come to be? This is, of course, a story in itself. In a sense, the development of the national parks has been a series of happy accidents, with the right person coming along at the right time with the right idea to help produce a system that is now the envy of the world. Today American citizens have come to treasure their parks to such an extent that only the most retrograde politician (and there have been a few!) would dare attempt to dismantle it.

Such was not always the case. Indeed, as historian Alfred Runte points out, politicians once promised that should a national park ever be needed for some more worthwhile purpose than "scenery," its authorizing legislation could always be rescinded. But that is only a part of the wonderfully checkered history of an idea—national parks—whose very origins are still in dispute. The critical event that started it all occurred either in the Dakota Territory in 1832 or in Arkansas in that same year, in California in 1864 or in the northwest corner of what is now Wyoming in 1872.

Possibly, we can trace the basic concept back even further—to 1810, in England's dramatically scenic Lake District, which poet William Wordsworth sought to preserve. This near-wilderness of mountains and glacial lakes and tarns should be declared, he wrote, "a sort of national property, in which every man has a right and interest who has an eye to perceive and a heart to enjoy." Wordsworth was offering a bold concept, for parks and preserves had traditionally been places of exclusion. There were city greens, commons, and pleasuring grounds, of course, but rural parks consisting of protected woodlands, moors, and trout streams were owned by or reserved for the use of kings, noblemen, and (later) moneyed aristocrats. Commoners were not allowed, and might even lose their heads for poaching or even trespassing. But after the Enlightenment, and especially after the great 18th-century republican revolutions in America and in France, ideas began to change. A national property—a national *park*—should be preserved not for the exclusive use of the privileged but for the benefit of the people.

Such an extraordinary idea seemed supremely logical to the American lawyer-turned-artist George Catlin, who, beginning in 1829, traveled west to paint Indians. As related by National Park Service historian Barry Mackintosh, it was on one of these expeditions, to the Dakota Territory in 1832, that Catlin became concerned about the impact of the advancing frontier on the Indians and on the wide-ranging wildlife—principally buffalo—upon which they depended. The Indian culture ought to be safeguarded, he argued, "by some great protecting policy of government…in a *magnificent park…a nation's park*," the emphasis being Catlin's own.

Meanwhile, that same year, a reserve, later to become a national park, was actually established by Congress—four square miles of Arkansas mountain land that contained "the Hot Springs of Washita," acquired in the Louisiana Purchase of 1803. Subsequently, opulent bath houses were built, some of them still in use, and the springs became known as "the National Spa." At length, Hot Springs, Arkansas, was declared the 18th national park in 1921. The town surrounding the park would become the boyhood home of President Bill Clinton.

Yet another claimant to the title of "first" is the Yosemite Valley of California, which, though not the first national park (it was, in fact, the fifth), was the first remote wilderness area to be given the kind of governmental pro-

Thomas Moran's *Grand Canyon of the Yellowstone*, 1872. Moran's paintings of the upper reaches of the Yellowstone River, which he visited in 1871, helped persuade Congress the following year to establish Yellowstone National Park, the first in a system that now numbers 368 units.

Selected Events in Park System History

Lewis and Clark Expedition, Missouri Breaks

• 1803 Louisiana Purchase.

• 1804–06 Lewis and Clark Expedition.

• 1819 Florida and other areas acquired in treaty with Spain.

• 1807 Yellowstone area discovered by John Coulter.

• 1810 Wordsworth describes England's scenic Lake District, offering concept of national property for the people.

• 1848 Mexican Cession of Texas and California.

• 1853 Gadsden Purchase of southern Arizona and New Mexico.

• 1871 Ha[...] Survey cor[...] description[...] Yellowston[...]

• 1872 Congress enacts leg[...] tion to cre[...] Yellowston[...] the first na[...] al park, e[...] passing 3,[...] square mi[...]

Geyser, Yellowstone

First rangers, Yosemite

• 1832 George Catlin suggests Indian culture of the Dakota Territory should be safeguarded "…in a magnificent park."

• 1832 Hot Springs of Washita, Arkansas, set aside as reserve.

• 1864 Ten square miles of Yosemite Valley granted to California for admiistration as a park, setting legal precedent for the first named national pa[...]

Admission to Statehood

Before 1790	*Before 1800*								
Connecticut	Kentucky						Florida		
Delaware	Tennessee	Ohio		Maine			Texas	Kansas	
Georgia	Vermont		Louisiana	Missouri	Arkansas		Iowa	West Virginia	Colorad[...]
Maryland			Indiana			Minnesota		Nevada	
Massachusetts									
New Hampshire					Michigan	Wisconsin			
New Jersey				Alabama		California	Oregon	Nebraska	
New York				Illinois					
North Carolina				Mississippi					
Pennsylvania									
Rhode Island									
South Carolina									
Virginia									

Wars

WAR OF 1812

CIVIL WAR 1861-65

Presidents

George Washington

John Adams

Thomas Jefferson

James Madison

James Monroe

John Quincy Adams

Andrew Jackson

Martin Van Buren

William Henry Harrison

John Tyler

James Knox Polk

Zachary Taylor

Millard Fillmore

Franklin Pierce

James Buchanan

Abraham Lincoln

Andrew Johnson

Ulysses S. Grant

Ruth[...]

• 1889 Casa Grande Indian ruins omes second national park.

• 1890 Sequoia established as third ational park.

• 1890 Kings Canyon (formerly amed General Grant) becomes urth national park.

• 1906 Antiquities Act provides penalties for disturbances or removal of an object of antiquity, resulting in the creation of national monuments.

• 1913 John Muir tries unsuccessfully to prevent flooding the Hetch Hetchy valley in Yosemite.

• 1899 Mount Rainier National Park, Washington.

• 1890 Yosemite becomes th national park.

• 1902 Crater Lake National Park, Oregon.

• 1916 Thirty-seven areas administered by Department of Interior; Organic Act sets up National Park Service, signed by President Wilson; first director is Stephen Mather.

• 1921 Hot Springs National Park, Arkansas.

• 1934 Great Smoky Mountains National Park, Tennessee and North Carolina.

• 1929 Horace Albright is chosen as second director of National Park Service.

Muir Woods, California

• 1933 As a result of Albright's "jump-seat lobbying" in the Shenandoah Valley, President F. D. Roosevelt issues two executive orders transferring 44 historic areas to the park service.

• 1940 Newton Drury is named park service's third director, and is able to limit wartime depredations and takeover of land for war effort.

• 1978 47 million acres in Alaska join system.

Eskimo family, Alaska

• 1955 Almost 200 parks are now in the system.

• 1964–68 23 historic areas are added to park system.

Utah   Oklahoma   Arizona
New Mexico

ning

Dakota
Dakota
ngton
ana

Alaska
Hawaii

Grover Cleveland

Theodore Roosevelt

Woodrow Wilson

Herbert Hoover

Harry S Truman

Lyndon B. Johnson

Gerald R. Ford

Ronald Reagan

nin
son

William McKinley

William Howard Taft

Warren G. Harding

Calvin Coolidge

Franklin Delano Roosevelt

Dwight D. Eisenhower

John F. Kennedy

Richard M. Nixon

Jimmy Carter

George Bush

Bill Clinton

George Catlin painted *Buffalo Bull's Back Fat, head chief, Blood Tribe*, in 1832. Catlin, a Pennsylvania lawyer-turned-artist, spent the 1830s painting portraits and tribal scenes of Plains Indians. Concerned about the fate of Native Americans, he proposed in 1832 a "nation's park" to protect them and their hunting grounds, and the artist was thus among the earliest to advance the national park idea.

tection called for by George Catlin. Granted to the state of California during the administration of Abraham Lincoln to be managed solely "for public use, resort and recreation…inalienable for all time," the 10-square-mile valley thus became the necessary legal precedent for the first *named* national park and for the 367 additional areas that were to follow.

That first park was, as many readers know, Yellowstone. We will discuss this park at greater length in a subsequent chapter, but it needs to be said here that the Yellowstone country was no ordinary hunk of Western wilderness. After the legendary John Colter, a soldier attached to the Lewis and Clark expedition of 1804, was given permission to go off on his own on the return trip from Oregon, he came upon the Yellowstone region, alone and afoot, in 1807, the first white man to do so. He returned to civilization with incredible tales of a smoking valley, of geysers, of bubbling, sulfurous pools, of giant animals and birds. "Colter's Hell" it was called, but scarcely anyone believed his stories or those of later explorers, such as mountain man Jim Bridger, who, after an 1857 trip to Yellowstone, became famous for his yarns about the place. After the close of the Civil War, government-sponsored scientific expeditions were mounted, culminating in the 1871 Hayden survey, which incontrovertibly confirmed that many of the tall tales were actually true. The following year, though not without heated congressional debate, legislation was enacted to create Yellowstone National Park from 3,300 square miles of public-domain land, most of it in the Wyoming Territory. The park was placed under the jurisdiction of the Secretary of the Interior, who was enjoined to "provide for the preservation, from injury or spoliation, of all timber, mineral deposits, natural curiosities, or wonders within said park, and their retention in their natural condition." No staff was available to the secretary to carry out this edict, and after a time the U.S. Army was asked to take on the job. That bit of history is honored today in the headgear of National Park Service employees—the old-time, creased campaign hats. They are worn proudly by what has become over the years an elite corps of dedi-

Ladies' hour at one of the "Hot Springs of Washita," now a part of Hot Springs National Park, Arkansas. Acquired by Jefferson in the Louisiana Purchase of 1803, Hot Springs lays claim to the title of the "oldest" park: although it was not given official park status until 1921, the area was set aside by Congress in 1832 as "the National Spa."

Park champion President Theodore Roosevelt (left) and conservationist John Muir at Yosemite. Yosemite was the fifth national park to be established (in 1890), but Yosemite Valley and its dramatic waterfall, seen in the background, had been protected by Congress in 1864, with management authority given to the state of California. Yosemite provided the necessary legal precedent for the creation of national parks by Congress, the first of which was Yellowstone in 1872.

cated men and women who protect and interpret such places as Yellowstone for tens of millions of visitors every year.

And so the great experiment in the creation of a national system of public parks was begun, although it grew quite slowly at first. Seventeen years passed; then the Indian ruins at Casa Grande, Arizona, were added in 1889, to be followed the next year by Sequoia, General Grant (later Kings Canyon), and Yosemite national parks in California. Mount Rainier in Washington came aboard in 1899, and Crater Lake, Oregon, in 1902. Perhaps the most striking characteristic of the debates surrounding the public decision to set aside such treasures was that in each case the argument turned on the "worthlessness" of the landscapes designated to be parks. The Yosemite Valley, said its proponent, Senator John Conness, of California, was "for all public purposes worthless," despite its scenic grandeur. Yellowstone was judged "so high above the sea" that it had no value for stock raising. Crater Lake, explained Congressman Thomas Tongue, of Oregon, who introduced park legislation in its behalf, was "a very small affair—only eighteen by twenty-two miles…no agricultural land of any kind."

Some have sought to explain these crass statements about our now-priceless national assets as a mere stratagem meant to assuage a few recalcitrant members of Congress. The idea of *worthlessness* does not comport well with the view, widely accepted, that the national park system was the result of great legislative statesmanship and a uniquely American ethical sensibility about scenic landscapes and indigenous cultures on the part of our political leadership. But such notions had no currency in the early days when the economic development of the West was a singular objective. "The worthless-lands speeches (in Congress) were no rhetorical ploys," Alfred Runte insists.

History on the Land

"They were, in fact, serious assessments of national park lands based substantially on the findings of government resource scientists." Indeed, had modern-day real-estate and tourism values been guessed at by early congressional sponsors, the great experiment might never have gotten off the ground. If anyone actually had a premonition of the value of these parks—as shoreline lots along Yellowstone Lake, say, or as board-feet of timber in the giant redwoods of the High Sierra—they kept mum about it.

Such were the contrary beginnings.

The next signal event, as perhaps befits this curious history, had nothing to do with national parks—at least not at first. But it provided an early clue that the system might one day be capable of encompassing the whole of the American experience, not just our fascination with nature's wonders, such as those found at Yellowstone. The event was the passage of the Antiquities Act of 1906, which, in the hands of President Theodore Roosevelt, provided a whole new direction in the progress of the national parks movement. The seemingly modest act had nothing to do with the withdrawal of land to protect the scenery, nor even to place any restrictions on its use. It was intended to provide penalties for the disturbance or removal of any object of antiquity, such as Indian ruins, instructing the government to preserve "all

Photographer William H. Jackson captured this image of the Ferdinand Hayden survey party as it entered Yellowstone in July 1871. The expedition, a rigorously scientific enterprise, finally persuaded Congress to believe the stories told by mountain men of the Yellowstone region. The geysers, vents of steam, and bubbling pools and cauldrons; the huge mammals and birds; and the towering peaks and rushing rivers were not trappers' tall tales.

objects of historic or scientific interest" on federally owned land. No congressional enactments were required to provide for such protection, as they were for national parks. Thus no arguments about "worthlessness" arose. Since the definition of "historic or scientific interest" could include almost any site, of any size, anywhere on federal land, Roosevelt had been handed a big stick. The result was the creation of what were to be called *national monuments*. Before he left office three years later, Roosevelt had established, by executive order, 18 of them. Theodore Roosevelt was not the only President to use this act freely, as we shall see. According to Barry Mackintosh, "nearly a quarter of the units of today's National Park System…sprang in whole or part from the Antiquities Act."

By 1916, the next date on our national parks time line, some 37 areas were being administered by the Interior Department as national parks, monuments, or reserves. But the department was scarcely up to the job. Several areas had to be farmed out to the U.S. Army—including Yellowstone, as mentioned, and the California parks. For the remainder, a hodgepodge of appointed administrators were placed in charge. The national monuments were largely ignored. The result was, in some cases, notably tragic. For example, in 1913, the city of San Francisco demanded that the beautiful Hetch Hetchy valley in the northwestern quadrant of Yosemite National Park be dammed to provide a water supply for the growing city. A spirited opposition

This 1872 photograph of the Hayden survey camp in Yellowstone includes, from left, William H. Holmes, artist; unknown man with rifle; F. H. Bradley, geologist; William H. Jackson, photographer; Jackson's assistant, C. R. Campbell; and A. C. Peale, mineralogist.

was mounted by John Muir and his fledgling Sierra Club, only to fail. The flooding of the valley to make a reservoir was "the worst disaster ever to come to any national park," in the view of the eminent park historian John Ise.

Accordingly, there was increasingly vocal support for setting up a special bureau within the Interior Department to manage, by means of a professional staff, this growing aggregation of "worthless" real estate. In 1914, Stephen T. Mather, a successful California businessman and college classmate of then Interior Secretary Franklin Lane, sent a letter of complaint to the department about the poor management at Yosemite. Wrote Lane in reply, "Dear Steve, If you don't like the way the national parks are run, come down to Washington and run them yourself."

The hard-charging Mather actually agreed—and what a piece of luck this was for the future of the parks. With Horace Albright, his 25-year-old second in command, Mather so firmly set the course and the tone of what was to be the National Park Service, as well as the direction of the national park system itself, that today it is almost as if these men were still overseeing operations themselves.

The "organic act" setting up the park service was signed in 1916 by President Woodrow Wilson, and Mather was appointed the first director. "By the way," said Secretary Lane to Mather, "I forgot to ask about your politics." He

The most famous geyser in the world, Old Faithful has captivated generations of visitors since Yellowstone National Park was born in 1872—a few years after William H. Jackson took this photograph, opposite. An 1871 steel engraving, published in the popular *Scribners Monthly*, conjures up a scene from Lieutenant Gustavus C. Doane's expedition to Yellowstone. The American public had become captivated both by the wonders of this region and the idea of its being designated a national park.

knew very well, of course, that Mather was an avid Republican and a heavy contributor to his party, which was not the party of Woodrow Wilson. The remark was Lane's way of saying that the directorship of the service was not a politically oriented appointment. No partisanship was to be allowed—except a partisanship for the parks themselves. This tradition has, with some exceptions, survived.

Mather's primary contribution did, in fact, require great political skill. What he set about to do was to counter the "worthless" lands concept by giving "value" to the parks. If the public perceived them as valuable, then Congress would value them, too. He enlisted the railroads to advertise the parks and to bring spur lines to them; and, based on the precedent in the 1864 Yosemite Park Act, he induced concessioners to establish lodges, campgrounds, and tourist services—many of which still continue. Writes Alfred Runte, "Confronted with the evidence that the national parks were capable of paying economic as well as emotional dividends, for the first time Congress had good reason to add to the system rather than dismantle it."

Although Great Smoky Mountain National Park, in North Carolina, was added during Mather's tenure, the system was essentially located in the far West. It was his deputy, Horace Albright, who sought to correct the imbalance: first in the language of the 1916 "organic act" itself, which he had helped draft (by including a specific reference to "historical objects"); and then, the year following, by urging that Civil War battlefields and other

Even before the turn of the century, tourists flocked to Yellowstone National Park, left. Above, Horace Albright (far left) and Stephen Mather (far right) appear in a 1925 photograph with White Sulphur Springs, Montana, resident Jimmie Johnson (next to Albright) and Charles Cook (next to Mather), an explorer of Yellowstone. Mather, the first director of the National Park Service, and Albright, his successor, firmly set the future course of the national parks.

Minerva Terrace, at Mammoth Hot Springs, Yellowstone, was formed by lime emitted in solution from hot springs hundreds of feet below the Earth's surface and deposited in the form of the mineral travertine.

historic sites then administered by the War Department be brought immediately into the national park system.

A history buff since his California childhood, Horace Albright visited Eastern battlefields and other historic areas on weekends after coming to Washington as a young lawyer in 1913, often in the company of other young government men who lived with him at the Washington YMCA. For 16 years he kept up the pressure for the War Department transfer, as deputy director and then as director of the National Park Service after Mather resigned in 1929, having suffered a debilitating stroke. Finally, on a trip organized in the spring of 1933 to take the newly inaugurated President Franklin Delano Roosevelt and a retinue of aides to visit Shenandoah National Park, in Virginia, which lay several hours' drive from the White House, he got his chance. On the way to the park, Albright was assigned to a car far to the rear of the President's. But once the motorcade arrived at former President Herbert Hoover's camp in the mountains—the property was to be deeded to the park—Albright, young, strapping, and enthusiastic, helped carry the polio-stricken FDR to the house. During the day's excursion, Albright told FDR

At Yellowstone, the sun sets over Firehole River in Midway Geyser Basin, below, and shoots steam from one of the park's many small geysers, opposite.

about the background of the Shenandoah park and of the development of a wonderful new scenic highway along the crest of the Blue Ridge.

As related in Albright's memoir, *The Birth of the National Park Service*, written with Robert Cahn, when it came time to leave, Roosevelt ordered his Secret Service chief: "Put me in one of those touring cars, and let Eleanor pick up somebody else to take back. I want Albright in the jump seat." And it was from that perch, inches from Roosevelt's ear, that Albright strongly suggested that the historical parks be transferred from the War Department to the National Park Service and that more such parks be added. "I was thunderstruck," Albright wrote many years later, "as he [FDR] laughingly ordered me, 'Get busy. Suppose you do something tomorrow about this.'"

And so, at last, the compass was boxed—with a national system that could have units in every part of the country of such a grand variety that no aspect of American cultural and natural history need be excluded. The pattern for our present-day ability to read the nation's history on the land was set. Two executive orders resulting from Albright's jump-seat lobbying

Giant sequoias of the Parker group tower 250 feet and more in Sequoia National Park's Giant Forest grove.

brought not only the War Department's historic sites into the fold but also national monuments administered by the U.S. Forest Service, part of the Department of Agriculture. As a result, 44 historic areas, many of them located in Eastern states (and including the National Capital Parks), were added to the park system. It was, Mackintosh writes, "arguably the most significant event in the evolution of the National Park Service."

Albright was also responsible for the present-day emphasis on "interpretation" in the parks. While concessioners, and in the case of early Yellowstone even the U.S. Army, provided "cone talks" as Albright termed them, the interpretive side of the park service's mission was haphazard at the outset. While superintendent at Yellowstone (as well as chief assistant to Mather), Albright established the position of "park naturalist." Later, as director, he created an education division as a major, co-equal branch of the park service. His prescription for the educational mission of the park service was that there should be "simple, understandable interpretation of the major features of each park to the public by means of field trips, lectures, exhibits, and lit-

A pool reflects sun-drenched clouds overhead in the Sierra Nevada, Sequoia National Park, California.

Opposite, vistas of pure brilliance: Cathedral Rocks at Yosemite, top left; Kings River in Kings Canyon National Park, California, top right; and Crater Lake, Oregon. Viewed from the Tatoosh Range, Mount Rainier, left, rises majestically from Mount Rainier National Park, Washington.

erature; emphasis on leading the visitor to study the real thing itself rather than depending on second-hand information; [and the] utilization of highly-trained personnel." The prescription has been followed ever since.

Hundreds of parks of every kind were to be incorporated under a succession of directors, many of whom were nearly as vivid as Mather and Albright. And the happy accidents continued. One involved the organization of the Civilian Conservation Corps to provide jobs for unemployed youth during the Great Depression. The "CCC boys," as they came to be known, built roads, campgrounds, and other facilities for the parks. The park service oversaw some 600 CCC camps, and the regional offices set up for this purpose evolved into the regional administrative structure the park service uses to this day.

With the advent of World War II, the CCC boys enlisted or soon were drafted, and the program was abandoned. And suddenly the parks were

vulnerable to resource exploitation as they had not been since Mather established the National Park Service. Miners, loggers, and others saw the need for wartime production as an opportunity to raid resources in areas heretofore protected by national park status.

Then, once again, just the right man at just the right time became director of the national parks—Newton Drury, a highly principled and courageous conservationist who is credited with saving the system from wartime depredation in the name of patriotism. Still, the parks went to war in their own way. Temporary office buildings were erected on the greensward around the Washington Monument in the District of Columbia; a mountain-warfare training camp was established at Mount Rainier National Park; and the hotel at Yosemite (among other parks) was taken over by the War Department to provide R & R for battle-weary servicemen.

After the war, with growing postwar affluence during the 1950s and '60s, came new problems, new characters, and a slew of new parks—nearly a hundred of them, ranging from the Saugus Iron Works National Historical Site, in Massachusetts, to Redwood National Park, in California. Key figures during this period were Stewart Udall, a conservation-oriented Secretary of the Interior rivaled only by Harold Ickes in devotion to the parks, and two park directors, Conrad Wirth and George B. Hartzog, Jr., who carried out the mandate for more parks in those years, including, during Hartzog's term, a special emphasis on historic parks. Twenty-three historic areas were added between 1964 and 1968 alone.

Hartzog, appointed by the Lyndon Johnson administration, stayed on during the first Nixon administration. And the director tried mightily to keep out of partisan politics, following the edict of Franklin Lane to Stephen Mather. Nevertheless he made a fatal error by denying special yacht-docking privileges at Key Biscayne to industrialist Bebe Rebozo, a close friend and financial supporter of President Richard Nixon. As a result, as Hartzog tells it in his biography, *Battling for the National Parks*, he wound up on Nixon's notorious enemies list and was summarily fired in 1972. Reflecting on this event, Hartzog writes that the great contribution of Stephen Mather and Horace Albright was not that they "removed the director's job from politics." Far from it. They, like Hartzog himself, "put the politics *into* the director's job," so that the politics would *stop* there, not begin there.

One more major dot on the national-park historical time line remains, and politics plays a role here, too: the eleventh-hour effort to withdraw from development or from devolution to the state and Indian tribes (as provided for by the Alaska Native Claims Settlement Act) large parcels of wilderness land in Alaska, and to give those parcels national-park status. The struggle over the amount and location of the land that should be devoted to parks in Alaska went on for seven years—between 1971 and 1978—with a coalition of national conservation organizations providing leadership on one side and the combined forces of resource-extraction industries—oil, minerals, tim-

Dusk settles over Great Smoky Mountains National Park, along the North Carolina-Tennessee border. The name *Smoky* refers to the blue smokelike haze that envelops the mountains, generated by the coniferous trees themselves.

Below, a hardwood forest near Little Pigeon River, on the Tennessee side of Great Smoky Mountains National Park. Opposite, Dark Hollow Falls cascades through ancient rocks at Shenandoah National Park, in the Blue Ridge Mountains of Virginia.

ber—and the state's congressional delegation on the other. When it looked as if no compromise would be possible, just before the deadline of midnight, December 18, 1978, President Jimmy Carter, under the authority afforded by the Antiquities Act of 1906, designated many of the areas conservationists had been lobbying for as national *monuments*, which later could be converted to national parks by congressional action. In the end, 47 million acres of Alaskan wilderness joined the national park system. In a state where once there had been only five park areas, now there were 24.

However much of the success of the national parks movement has depended upon fortuitous circumstance—that is, pure luck—as opposed to purposeful strategic planning, is a matter of conjecture or argument. But the fact remains that the establishment of our national park system has been one of the most brilliant domestic-policy achievements, ever, of the United States government.

Yes, the national park system today has its troubles. Too many people want to go to the same parks at the same time. Too little money is devoted to maintenance and interpretation. Urban encroachments affect even the remotest parks, such as Grand Canyon, now beset by air pollution from power-generating plants. Matters such as these will be discussed, as appropriate, in subsequent chapters. For the most part, though, this is a book of celebration. No death knell for the parks has sounded yet, and for the foreseeable future, at least, none will.

So let us go, then, on our tour—to read the history on the land as given us by all the people, past and present, responsible for this remarkable American institution, the national parks.

DISCOVER AMERICA

History on the Land

THE STORY IN THE AMERICAN EARTH

The flood comes, crawls thickly by, roaring
with self-applause, a loud
spongy smothering liquid avalanche:
great ant civilizations drown,
worlds go down,
trees go under, the mud bank breaks
and deep down underneath the bedrock shakes.

Edward Abbey
Desert Solitaire

W ere our years but milliseconds—that is, were we to live out our lives in geological time rather than in the quotidian minutes and hours of ordinary time—what we are pleased to call the "solid ground" would not be solid at all. We would be riding a trampoline that had been loosely mounted on a madly speeding truck.

Not long ago—at the beginning of the Mesozoic, a mere 225 million years past, which is not many for a four-and-a-half-billion-year-old planet— there was a single great continent called *Pangaea*. Gradually it split in two, with Laurasia on the north and Gondwanaland on the south, and the Tethys Sea in between. As time went on, further subdivision of this global real estate took place until, a hundred million years ago, the present-day continents were formed, each of them embedded in ever-shifting tectonic plates. (The word *tecton* in Greek means carpenter, or builder.) Seven major plates, including the North American plate, and 12 minor ones, constituting a *lithosphere* some 60 miles thick, now float hither and thither on a

Halls Creek Overlook, Capitol Reef National Park, Utah. This park contains the famed Waterpocket Fold, a wrinkle in the Earth's crust that stretches for 100 miles across south-central Utah.

matrix of semi-plastic goop called the *asthenosphere*, beneath which is the Earth's molten core.

In this process, which is called *continental drift*, those plants and animals living upon the North American plate back in Pangaea days, or their fossilized remains, have been moved thousands of miles. The magnetic poles have shifted, even reversed. And over the whole of Earth-time, both before Pangaea (what was before? a geographic mystery there!) and after, the climate has changed radically. Seas have come and seas have gone. Mountains have risen and washed away. Whole orders of creatures have appeared and disappeared. Great sheets of ice have covered parts of the continents and then receded. And then come again and receded again.

As for the North American plate, it has been simultaneously crashing into and pulling apart from others, especially the Pacific plate, which we shall deal with in a moment. And, among the myriad amazing outcomes, the crashes have created mountains, upwellings of the land, volcanism, earthquakes; the pullings apart have created oceanic rifts, trenches so deep that they are nearly devoid of life. Here is the truth: all this is happening *even as these words are written*. The mountains are still growing, rifts widening and deepening, weather changing, sediments accumulating and washing away, magma flowing, ice receding, seas rising—the Earth, withal, continuing to jounce us around from pillar to post. By the time you read these words, we will, every single one of us in North America, be located about an inch or two to the north and west.

For those brave souls who are fascinated by the lurching lithosphere and our place upon it, who are unafraid to confront the elemental and mysteri-

When the two great ghost continents of far antiquity—Laurasia and Gondwana-land—split apart, the realms that were to become Africa and Eurasia swung eastward to form the Eastern Hemisphere, also known as the Old World. Those that joined to shape North and South America stretched nearly from pole to pole, with a towering cordillera—a chain of mountain ranges—forming one backbone for the two New World continents. A mountain chain also linked the Old World lands, from Gibraltar in the west to China's Tien Shan in the East.

ous forces propelling our wild ride through geological time, and who wish to read this wonderful story in the American earth at first hand—welcome to the national parks!

Where else to begin but at the beginning? Do not breathe too deeply here, for the gases are poisonous. Do not get too close to rivers and fountains and lakes of fire: a misstep could be fatal, or at least cauterizing, for the heat is intense—2,000 degrees Fahrenheit. But if you are lucky enough to be present during an eruption, breathe anyway, get close enough to see. There in the fuming, hot-orange magma are the origins—the liquid essence of the big bang, which, after the swirling gasses cooled, coalesced like a poached egg to make Mother Earth.

We are at **Hawaii Volcanoes National Park**. Nowhere on the planet, at least not at this moment in geological time, can you so intimately observe

A fountain of fire erupts on Kilauea in Hawaii Volcanoes National Park on the Big Island of Hawaii. Scores of volcanic eruptions have seared Kilauea, including a series of ongoing "fountaining" episodes that began in 1983.

what it was like as the Earth's primary, continental landforms were created. In 1983, an eruption commenced in a rift zone of Kilauea mountain to demonstrate this primordial drama, and it shows no signs of abating. At times the volcanism is quiescent, but quite often not, for 47 separate "fountaining" episodes have occurred since January of 1983. Thus, with a little luck, one's visit may coincide with something spectacular, in which case it's a bit like having a ringside seat at the Creation. Geysers of searing magma, curtains of fire, spurt skyward 100 feet or more, sometimes to 1,500 feet. Lakes of lava appear; rivers of molten rock roll down into the sea, obliterating everything in their path, including houses and roads, sending up clouds of acidified steam as they plunge into the salty ocean waters. New peninsulas materialize; the island grows. A dozen years ago, a little cinder cone that volcanologists called the "O-vent" was just barely discernible above the surface of the ground on the flank of Kilauea, the smallest of the mountains on the island of Hawaii. The O-vent is now a kind of mountain itself—Puu Oo—some 850 feet high, a mountain on a mountain. Because of it, Kilauea may, in time, outgrow her sisters, Mauna Loa and Mauna Kea, the world's highest mountains when measured from their base. They rise 30,000 feet from the sea floor to their topmost rims, which are nearly 14,000 feet above sea level, 10,000 feet higher than the crater at Kilauea.

Though Mauna Loa is a still-active volcano, erupting 17 times in the last hundred years, it is Kilauea that is now the source of all the excitement, caused by the awakening of a goddess named Pele, "the woman who devours the Earth." In the mists of long ago in Hawaiian legend, Pele journeyed down the chain of Hawaiian Islands looking for a home, finally coming to

A geological time-scale chart depicts graphically the relationships of the eras, periods, and epochs discussed in this chapter.

				600
EONS	Cryptozoic (Greek for "hidden life") represents 90% of the estimated 4.6 billion years of Earth's history.			
ERAS	Precambrian			
PERIODS				Cambrian

		65	60	
EPOCHS	Because of the relatively short time span of the Cenozoic era, (only 7 million years) the Epochs of the Tertiary and Quaternary periods are shown in exaggerated scale. The Tertiary-period epochs are at 10 times' scale. Otherwise, if shown at the same scale as the rest of the chart, the Paleocene's 10 million years would be represented by a space less than 1/8" wide. The Quaternary-period's epochs are expanded out to 100 times' scale.		Paleocene	

her place in the crater Halemaumau at the top of Kilauea. Scarcely a million years old, the "Big Island," as Hawaii is called, lies at the southeastern end of the chain of islands, each younger than the next, as they arc in a long southeasterly line some 1,500 miles across the mid-Pacific. Pele's golden hair, which is natural spun glass, may be found in the smooth, hot-fudge swirls of cooled pahoehoe lava; her tears glint in the sharp, cinder-like aa lava (pronounced AH-ah). These two kinds of lava look altogether different but, formed under different conditions, have the same chemical composition: they are both created by Pele.

Those who prefer hard science to tales of Hawaiian volcanic goddesses (however metaphorically apt the legend of Pele turns out to be) may be more satisfied by a geological explanation of the volcanism that created the Hawaiian Islands in general and Kilauea in particular. The origin is a "hot spot," more or less permanently located beneath the Pacific plate at between 19 and 20 degrees latitude and 155 and 156 degrees longitude. As the plate has moved across this locus of asthenospheric violence—at a rate of three to four inches a year—great eruptions have ensued. At first, nothing could be seen above the surface of the sea, for volcanoes take eons to build their mountains. And then, at the very place where the Big Island is now located, Kauai, the oldest of the major Hawaiian Islands, appeared about five million years ago. And then the next, and the next, and the next—Oahu, Molokai, Maui—as the plate moved inexorably to the northwest. In time, the Big Island, and Kilauea with it, will also slide past the hot spot, and Pele's restless journey will resume. Perhaps her next destination will be Loihi Seamount, an underwater volcano situated 20 miles to the southeast of Kilauea. But

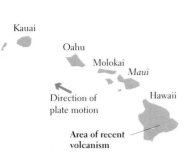

As the Pacific tectonic plate drifted to the north and west at the rate of three to four inches a year, a "hot spot" beneath the plate created the volcanic chain of islands we call Hawaii, above, beginning some five million years ago and continuing today.

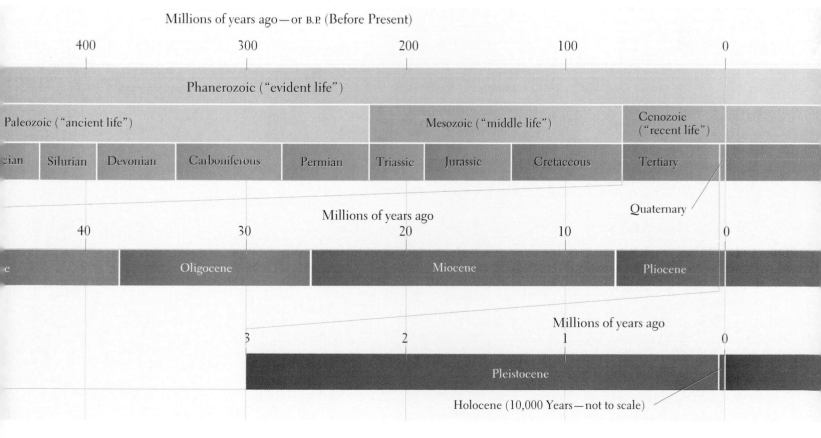

there is no need to rush to Hawaii to witness this event. Loihi is not likely to be seen above the waves for another 200,000 years—if ever.

Before about 1960, which is to say before the theory of plate tectonics was generally accepted by the scientific community, most geologists believed that the volcanism that created the Hawaiian Islands was caused by a rift in the seabed. That explanation was abandoned when it was seen that the islands are pretty much in the middle of the giant Pacific plate. Where this plate meets other plates, on the west the Eurasian plate and on the east the North American plate, is what is called the "ring of fire," encircling the Pacific Ocean with Hawaii as a kind of bull's-eye not far from the midpoint. The ring defines the places where the plates have crashed together and pulled apart to create giant, transforming seismic activity and volcanoes, including Mount Fuji in Japan, Mount Pinatubo in the Philippines, Mount St. Helens in the state of Washington; and Lassen Peak in California. All of these but Fuji have erupted in this century—two of them, Pinatubo and Mount St. Helens, quite recently. Lassen Peak last blew in 1914. It is now a national park itself.

Although a major earthquake hit Japan early in 1995, killing thousands, the volcanoes around the ring of fire are relatively quiet now, even Pinatubo, whose monstrous blast changed the weather patterns of the world for sever-

Fog enshrouds Kaluu o Ka Do and Kamaolii cinder cones at Haleakala National Park, Maui. Haleakala crater, which constitutes most of the park, is now a cool, cone-studded reminder of a once-active volcano.

al years. But Pele is still at work in a major way at Hawaii Volcanoes National Park, where she reveals some of the secrets, to all who might wish to learn of them, of how Mother Earth was made.

In 1957, a group of scientists calling themselves the American Miscellaneous Society decided that more should be known about the boundary between the Earth's crust, upon which we live (and oceans lie), and the mantle—the strata reaching down through the lithosphere to the plastic asthenosphere upon which the more solid material rests, albeit quite restlessly. How is it, among other questions the miscellaneous scientists wished to ask, that the Pacific hot spot formed? To help answer such questions, they decided to drill a hole right straight down into the earth to the boundary layer between crust and mantle—the "Mohorovičić discontinuity," familiarly known as the Moho. Thus was the Mohole project begun, off the coast of California, where the scientists believed the whole geological record of the Earth could be brought to the surface and studied. But less was learned than was hoped,

The Mauna Ulu lava shield at Hawaii Volcanoes National Park was created by eruptions between 1969 and 1974. Ropy, swirled lava such as that seen here is known as pahoehoe; another type, called aa, is chemically the same, but is jagged and sharp.

The ohia-hapuu tree-fern forest lies only a few miles away from the Mauna Ulu lava shield, and depicts life's ability to return to devastated areas. More than 90 percent of Hawaii's native plant and animal species are endemic, having evolved into species found nowhere else on Earth.

and the costs were greater than anyone had imagined. In 1966, the Mohole project was abandoned, proving, among other things, that the Earth gives up her secrets grudgingly.

Yet where technology failed to expose a complete geological record of the Earth, nature has succeeded in producing a partial one. And spectacularly so. The "Mohorovičić discontinuity" is not reached here, but you can find the Great Unconformity, as revealed by a rock formation that is 1.7 billion years old. This formation, called the Vishnu schist, above which rise the rainbow layers of sedimentary rock, lies 5,000 feet below the canyon rim—almost straight down—at **Grand Canyon National Park**. The walls of the canyon, recording the rise and fall of mountains and seas in their layered strata over a time incomprehensible to us, are, as nature writer Joseph Wood Krutch puts it, "the most revealing single page of earth's history anywhere open on the face of the globe."

The canyon itself defies description, but many writers have taken a crack at it anyway. On August 14, 1869, its first official American explorer, John Wesley Powell, wrote this diary entry, from the perspective of the Colorado River at the bottom of the canyon: "Up through granite crags…steep slopes

and perpendicular cliffs rise, one above the other, to the summit. The gorge is black and narrow below, red and gray and flaring above, with crags and angular projections on the walls, which, cut in many places by side canyons, seem to be a vast wilderness of rocks." Later he wrote: "One might imagine that this was intended for the library of the gods; and so it was. The shelves are not for books but form the stony leaves of one great book. He who would read the language of the universe may dig out letters here and there, and with them spell words, and read, in a slow and imperfect way, but still so as to understand a little, the story of creation."

From the perspective of the canyon *rim*, visitors are often offered the well-worn yarn of the young cowboy, who, having never heard that there was such a gigantic interruption in the flattish rangeland and stunted pinyon-pine forests of the region, reined in at the precipitous edge, saying, "Whoa, ol' hoss. Something big has happened here."

And if you ask the National Park Service rangers for *their* perspective, they will tell you that the canyon is 277 miles long, a vertical mile deep, and, at Grand Canyon Village, 10 miles wide, though at some places it is as much as 18 miles wide. They will tell you that nearly five million people visit here

Washington's Mount St. Helens rises serenely among the Cascade Mountains of the Pacific Northwest. On May 18, 1980, after a 123-year slumber, the volcano erupted, blasting some 275 million tons of earth skyward.

every year. And yet, withal, as Krutch points out, this is a place of solitude where human society, though present, seems irrelevant.

For those who can manage the trip—on mule back (expensive) or on foot (strenuous)—an excursion down into the canyon along a rim-to-river trail is the only way to get past the sheer *scenery* of the place and into its history, though there are many who are plenty satisfied with the scenery and return for vacation after vacation never once descending the steep trails beneath the rim. But the history has its beauty, too, even at the small scale of the fossil remains embedded in the layered rock—Major Powell's library.

At the cliff edge, the topmost strata is the whitish Kaibab limestone, sandy with the feel of the sea that most recently returned to make its deposits of the myriad creatures of warm waters 250 million years ago. This occurred long before dinosaurs, creatures of the Mesozoic era, which we shall be discussing presently. At the Grand Canyon, we are in the Paleozoic era. (*Paleo* means ancient; *zoic* means animal. *Meso* means middle.) Here at the close of the Paleozoic in the canyon's topmost stratum are mollusks of many kinds—the shellfish—along with ancient plantlike animals called sea lilies and feather stars that took their living by feeding on detritus; and brachiopods, of which there are 12,000 extinct species, and which are like bivalve mollusks, but then again not like them at all.

Next, just below the Kaibab limestone on the canyon's walls, is the Toroweap formation of sandstones and limestones, recording an earlier sea. Corals are found here, and bryozoans. Yet farther down, and further back in time, the hiker comes upon cream-colored Coconino sandstone, signifying that a great desert—like the Gobi or the Sahara—once covered the region. Some fossilized reptile tracks are found here, but no fossils of the animals themselves. Down a few hundred feet farther we come upon a swampland revealed by the Hermit shale and the Supai group of shales showing plant fossils and mud cracks. Where a few feet above us the place was dry and sandy, here the stone reveals a hot and humid climate, filled with insects. The earth-rock we dig at with a sharp stone picked up from the trail is now 300 million years old.

We move on, and even more limestone strata appear—Redwall, Temple Butte, and Muav, in red, orange, and white—showing that more seas have come and gone. Soon we arrive at a place where the stratum we examine is more than half a billion years old: the greenish Bright Angel shale of the middle-Cambrian period. Trilobite fossils, the quarry of every Geology 101 student in the land, may be found here, along with the remains of brachiopods and marine worms. Then comes the reddish Tapeats sandstone laid down by early-Cambrian seas, and we arrive at the cusp of the Great Discontinuity, the term having been invented by Powell to describe the spot where ancient, upended strata meet the level strata of the seas and swamps and sandy deserts we have just passed by. The discontinuous layers are a mix of pre-Cambrian rock, shales, and sandstones interleaved with lavas, laid down before the "Cambrian explosion" of complex life forms appeared. The formation as a whole, called the Grand Canyon supergroup, was tilted by a period of mountain-building, and then eroded flat over millions of years so that the material deposited above it was in a discontinuous relationship to it.

The supergroup and the strata above both lie upon the Vishnu schist. Named for the primary god of Hinduism, this rock formation, studded with garnets and other crystals and laced with once-molten granitic intrusions, was metamorphosed into a dark, fancifully swirled mass by means of great pressure and heat over billions of years. Upon reaching the Vishnu schist, we have come to the bottom of the canyon. It is morning. We have hiked down toward the beginning of life on Earth.

And yet the river is young—at work for only six million years in shaping the landscape of the canyon. How did the Colorado get way down here? The short answer is that it didn't. (The long answer has many complexities and mysteries that are still in dispute.) The elevation of the river has been roughly the same over its short life. Instead, after the river came into being (actually there may have been two rivers, one capturing the other), the land rose. During the Paleozoic era, when all those layers of silt and sand and mud were being deposited, Western America was devoid of mountains, being instead a flat, low-lying plain, at or somewhat below sea level. Then, inexorably, as the tectonic plates moved, the Pacific plate slid under the North American plate, raising the flat land now called the Colorado Plateau a mile

The sun illuminates the Grand Canyon's Mount Hayden, with Point Imperial on the North Rim in the background. Major John Wesley Powell, explorer of the Grand Canyon, called the strata revealed by this great declivity "the library of the gods." In the layers upon layers of rock, we can read much of Earth's history.

A Grand Canyon gallery hints at this formation's matchless beauty. Season after season, the land has risen as the Colorado River cuts down through the sediments deposited by the comings and goings of seas since the first stirrings of life on Earth. Yet the river itself is young, only six million years old.

Sunset at Hopi Point on the South Rim of the Grand Canyon. Nearly five million people visit this national park every year. Yet, as nature writer Joseph Wood Krutch has pointed out, it is a place of vast solitude, where human society, though present, seems irrelevant.

An aerial view of the Yampa River, opposite, portrays a section of the real "Jurassic Park"—Dinosaur National Monument, located astride the Colorado-Utah border. Giant creatures— some of them 70 feet long—once roamed the region.

above its original elevation and, in the process, creating the Rocky Mountains, which in turn fed vastly increased quantities of water into the river channel. All of this was, over the six million years, exquisitely orchestrated so that the once-meandering river (beginning life as a minor stream) would not spill out of its banks to seek a shorter route to the sea. The land rose, the water volume increased, and in time the great canyon was inevitably carved by the tumbling rock and sand and gravel of the Colorado River and its tributaries. And the carving is still going on. The land rises, the river deepens, the notch through which the waters pass widens and curves and ramifies, the boulders roll, obeying a law that decrees that, as Krutch puts it, "the transporting power of a given stream varies as the sixth power of its speed." This impressive geometry means that fast rivers like the Colorado can transport objects of stupendous, logic-defying size.

A tribe of Indians, the Havasupai, live within the vast canyon. But this is not a place that can be defined by human settlement, either by the big hotels along the rim or by the native dwellings below. The Grand Canyon is about time—time that is measured in the coming and going of great seas, in the movement of tectonic plates, in the building of high mountain ranges, in the grinding waters that grind on no matter what.

Yes, there *is* a "Jurassic Park" in our national park system. You have seen the movie; you can see the real thing at **Dinosaur National Monument**. The monument contains one of the largest deposits of fossil dinosaur bones yet found anywhere on Earth.

The dinosaurs appeared during the Mesozoic era, and lived on Earth for 160 million years—from 225 million to 65 million years ago. (By way of gaining some perspective on this number, it is well to remember that hominid species, of which *Homo sapiens* is the latest to evolve, have been around for less than five million years.)

At first the various dinosaur species were comparatively small. Then, as the Jurassic period of the Mesozoic unfolded, they began to reach the immense size that we commonly imagine when the word *dinosaur* is used: *dino* meaning terrible, and *saur* meaning lizard, although they are no more lizardlike than a great white shark is like a guppy. The lizard scurries about, low to the ground, but many dinosaurs became large, upright creatures, an adaptation that expanded their food supply by several orders of magnitude— from ground-level grasses and forbs to treetop leaves—leading to the great success of an animal order that became totally dominant the world over. Indeed, were it not for a great cataclysm at the end of the Mesozoic, about which more in a moment, the dinosaurs might be dominant even today.

Dinosaurs survive, but only in their bones, which, through science and the exercise of the human imagination, permit their reconstruction. And our imagination can be wonderfully engaged at Dinosaur National Monument, where, beneath the sheltering glass roof of a 150-foot gallery, the remains of some of the largest of the Jurassic creatures lie partially embedded, partially revealed, in a sharply tilted, almost upright slab of sandstone called the Morrison formation, which was laid down some 150 million years ago. Here, in

the bed of a meandering river, the skeletons of large numbers of dinosaurs came to rest.

The discoverer of this prehistoric ossuary was paleontologist Earl Douglass, who had been commissioned by Andrew Carnegie to find "something big" to feature in the philanthropist's new Carnegie Museum, in Pittsburgh. Douglass was able to meet that challenge and then some. His first discovery, in 1907, was of a six-foot-long dinosaur thighbone along the Green River, in Utah, a find that encouraged him to investigate the river basin more thoroughly. In 1909, he found eight large vertebrae of a *Brontosaurus* (since renamed *Apatosaurus*), and later came upon great quantities of bones and skeletons, piled up upon one another in giant windows.

In the course of these excavations, of which the Smithsonian Institution was an early sponsor, the largest specimen of the *Apatosaur* species was found, measuring 70 feet in length and 15 feet tall at the hips, with a high-soaring neck and head. Also found were many skeletons of the bizarre *Stegosaurus*, with its huge, finlike back plates, four-spiked tail, and tiny head, with a brain cavity so small it would scarcely accommodate a walnut. Mostly, the species found in the Morrison formation were herbivores. The world would have to wait for the next geological period of the Mesozoic era—the Cretaceous—to begin before the nasty *Tyrannosaurus rex* would evolve. Still, Douglass did come across a fine specimen of *Allosaurus*, a predatory beast of two and a half tons that was 30 feet long and equipped with a massive set of flesh-tearing fangs. In all, 10 species of dinosaurs were soon uncovered within what is called the "quarry site." Nothing new to science was

Scientists excavate dinosaur fossils in 1955 at Dinosaur National Monument's "quarry site," which was discovered by paleontologist Earl Douglass in 1909 when he found about 10 dinosaur species in a small section of tilted sandstone. It was Douglass's dream that the fossils be only partially excavated so that visitors could see them in place. In time, a glass gallery was built to protect a portion of the site, opposite, thus fulfilling Douglass's wishes.

The Story in the American Earth

found, but the quantity and quality of the remains of these giant Jurassic creatures were, and are, unsurpassed anywhere in North America.

It was Douglass's dream that an exposed section of the Morrison formation—where the greatest profusion of skeletons and their parts could be seen—be only partly excavated, so that the bones could be shown *in place*. In time, his dream became a reality: today, some 2,000 fossil bones lie revealed in a nearly vertical rock face of Morrison sandstone beneath the glass gallery, which is also the monument's visitor center.

In this place of superlatives—a Jurassic fossil park that has the most and best of what that period of gigantism has to offer—another superlative was added quite recently. Something new *has* been found, after all—a heretofore unknown species of carnivorous dinosaur that is something like *Allosaurus* but quite different in many important particulars. This newest creature was discovered just a mile from the visitor center, in a rock face high up in a box canyon. Here, George Engelmann, a paleontologist at the University of Nebraska at Omaha, spotted parts of what was later shown to be a nearly perfect skeleton, with every bone in place save the skull, for which the search goes on. (Dinosaur skulls have ever been a problem to locate. So tenuously are they attached to neck vertebrae that the skulls are, even when found, often at such a remove from the remainder of the skeleton that paleontologists are rarely absolutely certain they have the right one.)

The new dinosaur, as yet unnamed, is bipedal, about 20 feet long, and with relatively slight bones. According to National Park Service paleontologist Daniel Chure, who is studying the skeleton as it is slowly being extricated from the extremely hard rock in which it is encased, this species was probably fast on its feet—a swift and possibly canny predator. No, it is not like the *velociraptors* in the Spielberg film, except perhaps in this one characteristic. Clearly, the new find at Dinosaur National Monument is of major importance to paleontology. This is real science, and it is serious and terrifically exciting. However distant from us a fossil skeleton may be in terms of years, the new creature now emerging from the sandstone seems more intimate and essentially *present* than any strip of Hollywood celluloid could depict (as perhaps Mr. Spielberg would agree), despite clever cinematography. The basic lesson from the earth in this unit of the national park system is simple. Nothing beats the real thing.

Sixty-five million years ago, at the end of the Cretaceous period of the Mesozoic age and the beginning of the Tertiary period of the Cenozoic age, a literally world-shaking event took place. According to a hypothesis first propounded by physicist Luis Alvarez in 1980, a great meteor six miles in diameter struck the Earth, possibly on the Yucatán peninsula of Mexico, sending up gigantic, planet-enveloping clouds of particulate matter, acidi-

The eroded mudstone landscape of Badlands National Park, in South Dakota. Concealed within the layers of soft rock are fossils of strange creatures from the beginnings of the Age of Mammals. Sometimes visitors rather than scientists discover the fossil remains of these long-extinct forms.

This fossilized palm frond was found in the shale of Fossil Butte National Monument, in Wyoming, site of an ancient lake dating back some 50 million years.

fied vapors, and toxic chemicals. So great was the impact, many scientists now believe, that the Earth must have gone into a protracted planetary shudder, setting off earthquakes, volcanoes, tidal waves, and unimaginable winds and storms. As a consequence, with ecosystems so utterly vanquished and food chains so totally destroyed in the endless darkness, many life forms that were not wiped out by the collision and its immediate aftermath eventually expired from extreme environmental changes. In the end, some 75 percent of all plant and animal species disappeared from the face of the Earth.

Among others, bugs, fishes, mollusks, worms, and certain kinds of plants survived. Also surviving the Cretaceous extinction were tiny rodentlike furry animals, which had the ability to regulate their own internal temperature and to nourish their live-born young with curious glands. Thus did the age of the giant dinosaurs end, their very success leading to their downfall, and the age of mammals begin, with a new set of creatures every bit as strange to us as those they supplanted. If you wish to find out about how these new creatures evolved, one of the best places to visit is a former mud flat in South Dakota that is now an almost dreamlike landscape located within **Badlands National Park**, the cradle of American paleontology.

The place doesn't look like the cradle of anything. "Hell with its fires burned out," General George A. Custer, who was to learn something of hell at Little Bighorn, once called it. In 1849, when geologist John Evans came into this lonely country, he described the badlands as a "city of the dead, where the labor and the genius of forgotten nations had left behind them a multitude of monuments." For Evans, the eroded mud-rock crenelations and spires and mazes seemed sculpted for some human purpose. Since then, artists and photographers, as well as ordinary sightseers, have found the fantastic forms, so suddenly opening up in a declivity of the flat Dakota prairie, a landscape of unsurpassed beauty. And that is true: this national park is worth a visit just for the look of it.

Even so, what the fanciful shapes and forms of the soft stone conceal is every bit as sensational as what they reveal. A few feet behind any mudstone wall (or siltstone or claystone—all are here) on which a visitor places his or her hand may lie the remains of, say, an *Oreodont*, a peculiar animal two to five feet long with 44 teeth plus short tusks, a kind of cross between a pig and a cow. Other possibilities: a *Protoceras*, a combination pig and sheep in which the male of the species sported five pairs of knobs or horns, all pointed in different directions; or a huge, rhinoceros-sized creature called a *Titanotheres*; or a saber-toothed tiger; or a small camel (which originated in North America some 40 million years ago); or a tiny creature, the size of a lap dog, with four toes on its front feet and three on its back feet, which for all the world looked like a horse—because it was.

Here, then, in this relatively confined area, is the record, buried in soft rock, of the rise of mammals. In fact, by 1859, when Charles Darwin's *The Origin of Species* was first published, paleontologists were well along in their exhumation of fossil mammals in the White River "bone beds," as they were then called. The discovery of several stages in the evolution of the horse at the Badlands provided, says Joseph Zarki, chief of interpretation at the park, "the smoking gun" that helped to validate Darwin's then-radical theories.

Above, the Niobrara River snakes through Agate Fossil Beds National Monument, Nebraska. The beds, so named for their proximity to rock formations containing agates, hold the fossilized remains of animals that lived in what was then a savanna during the Miocene epoch some 22 million years ago.

Carnegie Hill rises above Agate Fossil Beds National Monument. O. A. Peterson of the Carnegie Museum, in Pittsburgh, oversaw the first scientific excavation at the site in 1904.

The Story in the American Earth

Opposite, Blue Basin, in John Day Fossil Beds National Monument, Oregon. This river valley contains a remarkable 40-million-year fossil record of the diverse plant and animal life that existed here from 45 million to 5 million years ago. In the monument's Painted Hills, below, the weathering of volcanic ash under varying climatic conditions has resulted in vividly hued rock layers of red, pink, bronze, tan, and black.

When Yale University paleontologist O. C. Marsh published a paper on the fossil horses found at Badlands, Darwin himself thanked the American, stating that his work provided "the best support to the theory of evolution that has appeared in the last twenty years."

Fossils taken from the Badlands can now be seen in most major natural-history museums in the United States, including the Smithsonian. For the visitor to the park, an essential side trip is to the South Dakota School of Mines and Technology, in nearby Rapid City. The school's museum boasts the best collection of White River fossils in the country.

And new discoveries are still being made. In 1993, a reporter and a photographer on assignment for an Iowa newspaper came upon what looked to them to be a fossil vertebrae column that had been exposed after a heavy rain. The two men knew the rules: leave such specimens in place and report their location to the park rangers. As it turned out, the backbone they found was attached to an excellent specimen of *Archaeotherium*, a wild-boarlike mammal that lived 34 million years ago. Further excavation of the site also turned up the remains of ancient rhinoceroses and horses. The journalists had discovered, in fact, one of the most productive fossil beds in the Badlands region. Excavations continue there, and visitors can observe the paleontologists at work on what is now called "the Big Pig Dig."

What are the chances of happening across a fossil? A find like that of the Iowa journalists is rare, but bits and pieces of fossils (leave them in place!) can be revealed after any rainstorm, for the rocks are soft and easily eroded. Moreover, uninhibited exploration is possible here—and even encouraged by park officials. The effects of families scrambling around in the ravine mazes (where a half-dozen people get lost every year, though not seriously) or climbing up on the pillows and pinnacles of mudstone are quite temporary, for the next rain will wash away whatever marks the climbers may have made. Although the sedimentary layers of the badlands formations go back

The snowcapped Fairweather Range rises behind Bartlett Cove in Glacier Bay National Park and Preserve, Alaska.

Three hundred years ago, this was a scene of solid ice.

to the beginning of the Cretaceous epoch 66 million years ago, the erosion that has created the fanciful shapes and revealed the remains of so many amazing animals has been going on for only half a million years. And it will go on for only half a million more, until the sediments here, with their burden of bones, are washed away, and the land is rendered as flat and featureless as it was before.

Meanwhile, in this strange and challenging interruption in the vast short-grass prairies of the American West, the age of mammals continues. Modern species find sanctuary here—American bison, prairie dogs, black-footed ferrets (highly endangered and recently reintroduced to the park), bighorn sheep—inhabiting the grasslands yet to be eroded. Under their feet lie the fossil remains of their ancestors, unknown to them except in genetic codings. Human visitors know more, at least taxonomically—the phylum, class, order, family, genus, species. But great mysteries still abide, secreted behind mudstone walls.

Across most of North America are the landscape remnants of the most recent of the gigantic earth-shaping events of geological history—the Ice Age of the Pleistocene epoch of the Cenozoic era, which is *our* era. The Ice Age, beginning a million years ago, had its most recent retreat at 12,000 B.P. (before present time), and vivid evidences of this movement are everywhere to be found in the northern tier of the United States and down along the major mountain chains. These include striations on suburban boulders in Connecticut, monadnocks in Massachusetts, drumlins and eskers in Wisconsin, potholes in Nebraska, the Finger Lakes in New York, and the depressions creating the Great Lakes, as well as the beautiful Yosemite Valley in California's Sierra Nevada. Glacial till brought great distances from the north produced the largest, most fertile expanse of farmland on the face of the globe in the upper Middle West; and everywhere the glaciers—continental, coastal, or montane—shaped and reshaped the land, routed and re-routed the rivers, drained and refilled the lakes, and defined and redefined the shorelines.

Although present time has been assigned its own epoch, the Holocene (*holo* meaning everything, *cene* meaning recent), there is some question as to whether the Pleistocene is really over. Perhaps, some say, we are simply in an interglacial period, that the glaciers, though now retreating, will come again with their great power to move mountains, create great lakes, and produce a billion acres of topsoil. To get a sense of that power, it is not necessary to own a time machine for a trip back to the end of the last Ice Age or forward to the beginning of the next: we can see it any day of the week, at least during the summer, at **Glacier Bay National Park and Preserve**.

Here, in the fjords of the Alaska panhandle, a confluence of glaciers—12 of them—flow down the mountains and into the waters of the bay. In bright white ribbons of ice, hundreds of feet thick and (at the widest point) a mile and a half across, the glaciers move slowly but inexorably toward the sea, the product of snowfall in the Fairweather Range, which reaches an elevation of more than 15,000 feet. At this latitude and altitude, more snow

Fireweed flourishes along Glacier Bay's Bartlett Cove. The forest around the cove is about 200 years old. Farther up the bay, younger forests fill in behind retreating glaciers. Right, Glacier Bay's Lamplugh glacier. Tidewater glaciers flow down the mountainsides into the bay, a fjord that extends 65 miles inland from the sea. The park is not accessible by road, and is open only in summer. Even so, a quarter of a million people visit annually.

falls on the mountains than is melted, and so it accumulates, season after season, compressing itself first into névé, a heavy, coarse kind of snow, then, beneath the névé, into granular ice. The great mass, though not liquid, actually flows downhill as the compression builds, eventually traveling distances of 15 to 25 miles. Where the glacier fronts reach the bay, palisades of ice, tall as a 20-story building, sever themselves from the main body of the glacier and fall into the waters—"calving," it is called—with a thunderous roar, sending up great ebullitions of spray and creating a series of deep-rolling waves that set the floating ice into a violent, echoing dance. This is, one soon becomes aware, extraordinary geological theater.

The bay is something new, or at least newly revealed. Just 300 years ago, which is not long before the first European scientists (in George Vancouver's 1794 expedition) came to study the region, the bay was surmounted by a single, compact sheet of ice some four thousand feet thick. No bay could be discerned beneath the remnants of what glaciologists call the "Little Ice Age," which began 4,000 years ago. Since the 1700s, the glaciers of Glacier Bay have retreated 65 miles, uncovering a complex, two-armed water body with a profusion of steep-sided fjords ramifying from each of the arms. Moreover, with the release of the great weight of the ice on the Earth's crust in the region, the land has risen, with new islands appearing in the bay, some of them fairly sizable. This phenomenon is called isostatic rebound, and at Glacier Bay the rebound, combined with adjacent mountain-building, produces a

land-rise of about one and a half inches a year. In this century, therefore, the rise has been more than 10 feet.

In recent years, the glaciers' retreat has slowed, and perhaps stopped, with some of the glaciers beginning to advance again. Though the events may be unrelated to a general advance, some of the glaciers have been known to surge 300 feet in a single day, which for a glacier is Mach 1. The precise mechanisms of major interglacial retreats and advances are poorly understood, but the larger events relate to global climate change. One would think that the current period of global warming, which many scientists believe is a product in part of the "greenhouse effect" from excess carbon dioxide and other industrial-age gases being pumped into the atmosphere, would cause a further retreat of glaciers around the world. In fact, the reverse may be the case, since snowfall at the Earth's poles can increase with the warming, building up the thickness of the ice, which, in turn, causes glacial advance. Global warming may well have set off the last glacial event of the Pleistocene, creating the Wisconsin Ice Sheet, a continental glacier that began its retreat only 12,000 years ago.

It's not easy getting to Glacier Bay. No roads go there, only boats and airplanes. Moreover, it's not on the way to anyplace else—at least to anyplace most summer vacationers might wish to visit. Nevertheless, the park attracts a quarter of a million visitors each year, all in the summer. Once there, a family can economize by camping out, although it may be wet, for coastal rains are frequent. It is true that one can see the *effects* of glaciation in any number of places that are easier to get to, but nowhere else on this continent can glaciation-in-action be so intimately observed. The best kind of front-row seat, most agree, is a kayak floating in the bay—albeit at a respectful distance from the looming glacier faces. The cold, sub-arctic air is alive with the sounds of ice moving, of groans and creaks and sharp reports, as you glide among the bergs. You are, for a moment, a part of geological time, not the ordinary time of meetings, deadlines, and alarm clocks. When the ice-bells sound here at Glacier Bay, epochs are being recorded.

And so does our journey into the Earth come to an end, beginning with fire and ending with ice, framing long eras of tectonic convulsions, inexorable erosions, and the emergence of living creatures that defy the imagination. It is an almost godlike privilege to witness the Earth's creative forces so directly and personally—a privilege that is passing strange when one considers that our species is a quite recent, and perhaps anomalous, addition to the sun-struck planet that is our home.

But that is where the story goes next. To our own kind, and how we came to live upon a continent that evolved, for all but a tiny fraction of its history, without us.

Ice sculptures in Tarr Inlet, Glacier Bay
National Park and Preserve.

FIRST
FAMILIES
AND FELLOW
IMMIGRANTS

The land and the people hold memories, even
among the anthills and the angleworms, among
the toads and the woodroaches—among gravestone
writings rubbed out by the rain—they keep old
things that never grow old.

—Carl Sandburg
"Cornhuskers"

A million years or so ago, our immediate hominid predecessor, *Homo
erectus* (much like *Homo sapiens*, except with a somewhat smaller
brain), finally came out of Africa, where it and earlier hominid
species had been living for the previous three or four million years. At first
the people, if we may call them that (as perhaps we should), moved into
parts of Asia that had climates much like their own in the savannas of East
Africa. Then, about half a million years ago, a new species arose, *Homo sapiens*, a bit smarter than *Homo erectus*, along with a subspecies, *Homo sapiens
neanderthalensis*, which later died out. As humans evolved, they became
more skillful at adapting to harsher climates and exploiting varied food
sources. Accordingly, they proceeded farther afield into Europe and northern Asia, until at last they had populated much of the Eurasian land mass.

But what about the Western Hemisphere? How did people get *here*? And
when? In recent years, after sifting through a good bit of wildly varying evidence, scientists have begun to form something of a rough consensus, al-

The ruins of San Gregorio de Abò church
at Salinas Pueblo Missions National
Monument, New Mexico. On an expedition to investigate the Salinas district in
1853, U.S. Army Major J. H. Carleton
came upon Abò at dusk. "The tall ruins,"
he wrote, "standing there in solitude, had
an aspect of sadness and gloom."

though controversy over the details still rages. The story goes like this. By the time the hominids moved out of Africa, the continents had long since drifted to their present locations, which in effect isolated the Western Hemisphere from the rest of the world. The only place where a human migration into it might logically occur was where the continents were almost but not quite connected, in the far northeastern corner of Siberia. Here, a strait separated the land masses, although the waters were relatively shallow and the strait—presently only 55 miles wide—was narrow. But this would still have been enough to block the progress of even the sturdiest of human adventurers in those days.

Then a wonderful coincidence took place. During the late Pleistocene,

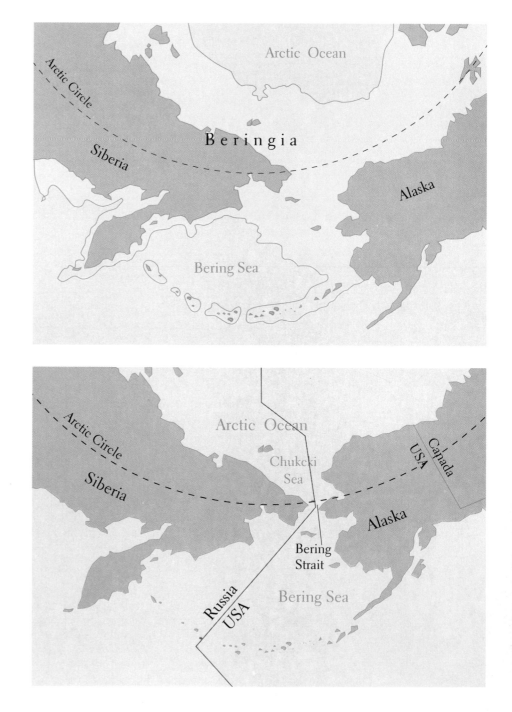

Some 20,000 years ago, immense glacial sheets covered much of the Arctic. With so much of the globe's water frozen, sea levels dropped 300 feet, exposing a land mass called Beringia, above. Beringia bridged the Eurasian and North American continents at the point where a 55-mile-wide strait, right, today separates Siberia from Alaska. This ancient "land bridge" enabled the first humans to migrate from the Old World to the New.

as human migrations approached western Siberia from Europe and Asia, arriving at about 20,000 B.P. (before present), great glaciers once again, as they had throughout the period, locked up a significant fraction of the seawater. As the seas lowered, a new land area, now called *Beringia*, emerged, connecting the two unconnected continents, Eurasia and America, just as humans arrived within striking distance of it. This area is called a "land bridge," although, at a thousand miles wide from north to south, it was more than just a bridge; it was an immense staging area for the inhabitation of a New World. But the staging area, Beringia, would not last forever. The geological window of opportunity provided by the emergence of Beringia was open only between 30,000 and 10,000 years ago, after which the waters would rise again.

Somehow the people made it in time so that the long trek southward down the continent could begin. Anthropologists now put this period of migration somewhere between 14,000 and 11,500 B.P., with the earlier date being somewhat problematic. The arrival time incontrovertibly confirmed by the carbon dating of the earliest known human artifacts (uncovered at Clovis, New Mexico) is 11,500 B.P. At Clovis, spear points of an unusual design were found, characterized by longitudinal grooves, or flutes, chipped onto the faces of the points. Such fluted "Clovis points" have been found at many sites throughout the Americas, and, remarkably, all date to around 11,500 B.P., suggesting the validity of that date of entry as well as the relatively rapid dispersal once humans arrived south of the ice sheets that then separated Beringia from the rest of the continent.

As for the area north of the ice sheets, anthropologists John F. Hoffecker, W. Roger Powers, and Ted Goebel discovered what they believe to be a Clovis-type "tool kit" in north-central Alaska dating to about 11,800 B.P., the first such find in this region. The near coincidence of dates (although some have raised doubts as to these relics being of the "Clovis" type) indicates that, if in Alaska, where the earliest evidence of human activity is likeliest to be found, the artifacts are not much older than in other proven sites of North

This Clovis point was unearthed in Colorado; such projectile points date to between 11,000 and 10,000 years ago. Although they have been found all over North America, Clovis points are named for the New Mexico site where they were first discovered in 1932.

Musk oxen on Nunivak Island, Alaska. During the Pleistocene epoch, the ancestors of these animals were present throughout the Arctic and may have been hunted by the first Americans.

America, then the chances are good that *Homo sapiens* was simply not present anywhere in the Western Hemisphere until that time. "The central Alaskan record indicates," Hoffecker and his colleagues write, "that the earliest documented occupants…entered the region during the 12,000 to 11,000 B.P. interstadial." (An "interstadial" is a period when glaciers are neither advancing nor retreating.)

Whether at 11,500 B.P. or a few thousand years earlier, the first families moved along Beringian stream valleys, hunting bison, elk, and other large mammals (including mammoth and other now-extinct "megafauna") as they went, and taking fish and small animals as well. In time, possibly quite soon after their arrival, some of the newcomers found a narrow, ice-free corridor between the coastal Cordilleran ice sheet and the continental Laurentide ice sheet that opened up at the end of the Ice Age and could provide them a passage southward into warmer climates and greater quantities and varieties of fish, game, fruits, nuts, grains, and edible plants and roots than their people had ever seen before.

So did we discover America.

Couldn't these migrants have arrived earlier than 11,500 years ago, or even 14,000? Couldn't they have come by some other route? Thor Heyerdahl, a Norwegian anthropologist, tried to prove—by taking such voyages himself—that early colonization could have succeeded by means of long ocean voyages in papyrus boats from the Mediterranean to the West Indies. Other ancient peoples might have rafted westward across the Pacific, suggesting that Polynesia was first settled by South Americans. Heyerdahl's ad-

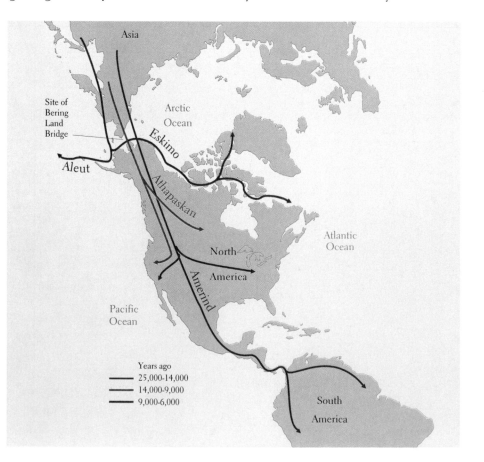

Humans crossed Beringia from Asia to enter North America about 12,000 years ago. Although relative latecomers to this fertile land mass, they spread rapidly eastward and southward over the Americas.

ventures produced several fascinating books (notably *Kon Tiki*), but such speculations have largely been laid to rest by archaeological evidence, as well as by new, and persuasive, physiological findings. Similarities in tooth structure and in many genetic markers in the blood between American Indians and northern Asiatics show quite recent common ancestry.

Even so, a few anthropologists still believe humans might have entered the continent much earlier, based on the discovery of apparent human artifacts in the Western Hemisphere located in strata dating back as far as 200,000 B.P. The trouble is that the finds suggesting very early migration have not held up to rigorous scientific scrutiny. Few archaeologists and anthropologists accept any evidence that dates the entry of humans into the Western Hemisphere prior to 14,000 B.P. Early humans simply would not have been able to get through the Cordilleran-Laurentide ice-sheet barrier, which was in place between 14,000 and 20,000 B.P. It is barely conceivable that they might have slipped across just prior to 20,000 B.P. (even though they had scarcely made it to Siberia). Once field and laboratory work is complete, a tantalizing site now being studied in Chile may imply that a 20,000 B.P. crossing is not out of the question. At this writing, however, 11,500 B.P. still stands as the earliest proven date of human occupation of areas south of the Pleistocene ice sheets.

As for Native Americans, whose tribal legends suggest origins other than the accepted one, many remain altogether unconvinced of this mainstream scientific thinking. In *America in 1492*, for example, noted author Vine Deloria, Jr., a Standing Rock Sioux, states: "The Bering Strait theory is tenaciously held by white scholars against the varied migration traditions of the

Smithsonian Arctic explorer Edward W. Nelson encountered these Inuit people, below, during the 1870s. Ancestors of the Inuit were the last pre-European immigrants to arrive on the North American continent.

Located in Denali National Park and Preserve, Alaska, Mount McKinley is the highest mountain in North America, its snowy summit reaching 20,320 feet above sea level. The Athabaskan people gave the name Denali, the "High One," to this massive peak.

natives and is an example of the triumph of doctrine over facts.... If the universities were controlled by the Indians, we would have an entirely different explanation of the peopling of the New World and it would be just as respectable for the scholarly establishment to support it."

It is, of course, possible that a new find may turn up somewhere that will knock accepted theories into a cocked hat, although perhaps not in such an extreme way as implied by Deloria, whose assertions are possibly offered more for rhetorical effect than as considered opinion. "This much is certain," writes anthropologist David J. Meltzer, of Southern Methodist University, in an authoritative round-up paper on the dispute, "the first Americans were *Homo sapiens* who came from northeast Asia via the Bering Straits....These hunter-gatherers were present throughout the Americas by 11,500 years ago, in time to witness the climatic and ecological changes, including the extinction of thirty-five genera of megafauna that signalled the end of the Pleistocene. Beyond those bare facts there is controversy." In a sense, then, we are all newcomers—at least so it would appear from the archaeological record. In terms of the span of human existence in Eurasia over hundreds of thousands of years and our evolution in East Africa over millions of years before that, the human occupation of the Western Hemisphere occurred practically yesterday.

It is thought that the earliest of the migrants, the Amerinds as they are called, constitute the bulk of the Paleo-Indian people who settled North and South America. They were followed soon after by the Athabaskan people, identified (like the Amerinds) by a common early language that connects the present-day Indians of Alaska and Greenland with the Navahos and the Apaches of the Southwest. The last of those coming from Siberia, the Aleuts and Eskimos, are said to have arrived by kayak 2,000 to 4,000 years ago, though some believe they may have predated the Athabaskans and walked into Beringia.

And then, just a few thousand years after the last of those we call Native Americans arrived, the people who journeyed here from the West were met in the New World by those who journeyed here from the East, beginning with Nordic explorers around A.D. 1000. Five hundred years later the advance detachments of great numbers of new immigrants began to arrive from other Old World countries for purposes of conquest and colonization. Unhappily, not all of this latter-day immigration was voluntary, nor were the newcomers respectful of those who had arrived here first. Perhaps the two most hideous effects of the imposition of European culture on that of the first immigrants was the introduction of smallpox, which within a few generations nearly wiped out the Indians, and the near extinction of the buffalo, which sustained the few tribes that were left freely roaming the plains. It has been said that smallpox was deliberately introduced into Indian settlements and encampments by Europeans once they realized how vulnerable the Indians were to it. And there is no doubt that the extirpation of the buffalo was at least in part a deliberate strategy. Only slavery ranks with these as tragedies of such historic magnitude.

But wherever the newcomers came from, and whenever their arrival happened to be, and whatever fate befell them, the different peoples who

First Families and Fellow Immigrants

immigrated into this previously unsettled and resource-rich continent created homes and communities and landscapes and cultures possessed of more intriguing variation than those in any other part of the world. And much of this diversity is preserved, protected, and interpreted by the national parks. From the spear points of the Clovis people to the cannons of the conquistadors, and from the caves of Archaic American Indians to the cabins of European homesteaders, the parks offer a dozen millennia of American heritage for us to discover.

With mountains of the 600-mile-long Alaska Range looming in the distance, autumn graces Denali National Park and Preserve's taiga, a Russian term for areas of scant tree growth meaning "land of little sticks." Most of Denali's taiga is found at lower elevations along rivers.

In tracing American cultural history via the national parks, it is, in fact, possible to go back to the beginning, to Beringia itself—or at least a nearly three-million-acre part of it that is still above water on the Seward Peninsula. The **Bering Land Bridge National Preserve** may, however, be even less hospitable to *Homo sapiens* than it was at the time of the first migrations. Instead of a steppe, a rolling grassland with a generally temperate climate, the preserve is now tundra, a boggy expanse laced by streams and dotted with small lakes, the whole of it underlaid by permafrost. Much of the old Beringia of 11,000 years ago lies 300 feet below the Arctic Ocean and the Bering Sea adjoining the preserve. Perhaps beneath these waters are archaeological secrets that could help us unlock the mysteries of the great Pleistocene migration.

Some 55 miles across the Bering Strait lies Siberia, Russia being our closest neighbor with whom we do not share a border. In fact, the neighborliness is closer than that. Little Diomede Island, U.S., situated about 25 miles from the Seward Peninsula's Cape Prince of Wales, is but three miles from Big Diomede Island, Russia, which lies an equivalent distance from Cape Dezhneva, on Siberia's Chukotsk Peninsula. After the end of the Cold War, it became permissible for the American Inuits (the name they prefer to Eskimo) to visit their relatives, the Russian Inuits. There is no difference in language, for the Inuit tongue is spoken in the polar North, without regard to national boundaries. Even so, dialects have developed that can often make it difficult for Inuits away from their own clans to make themselves understood. Great cultural similarities remain, however, and serve to bind the Inuits together. In 1990, President George Bush and President Mikhail Gorbachev agreed to work toward an international park that would encompass the preserve and a new Russian park to be established on the Chukotsk Peninsula. The idea is still awaiting legislative approval on both sides, and the National Park Service, in anticipation of eventual ratification, has begun an ecological and ethnographic research program.

Should you wish to visit the Bering Land Bridge National Preserve, just to stand on the very plain across which the earliest American families once journeyed, you must first fly to Nome (or Kotzebue), Alaska, and once there engage a bush pilot to deliver you to the preserve. In the preserve, visitors can lodge at one of six widely scattered shelter cabins (although these are primarily for emergency winter use) or at a bunkhouse located at Serpentine Hot Springs, about 80 airline miles north of Nome. The bunkhouse sleeps 15 to 20 people in two rooms—his and hers. There is no indoor plumbing, but the hot springs bubble year-round. In the summer, hats with mosquito netting must be worn. It is legal, says the park service, to carry firearms in the preserve for protection against grizzly bears and other large animals.

Many of the new arrivals on the Bering land mass did not stop to settle there but kept on going south. And they must have moved with some speed, or else how could it be that the Clovis points are found in various places throughout the hemisphere dated to approximately the same period? One explanation offered for the rapid dispersion of the Paleo-Indians is that they were following highly mobile big game—the so-called megafauna that some believe they hunted to extinction. Spear points have been found embedded in the skeletons of both mammoths and mastodons. Additional victims of what biologist E. O. Wilson calls "a hunter's blitzkrieg" lasting several centuries include the giant ground sloth, whose last known population lived in caves at the western end of the Grand Canyon, camels, huge bison, the saber-toothed cat, a giant beaverlike animal, and peccaries (wild pigs) of various sizes.

Although the only direct evidence of the wholesale slaughter necessary to extinguish the 35 genera that disappeared at the end of the Pleistocene are spear points found among the bones of two of them, the Paleo-Indians are generally blamed for the extinction. Quite recent analyses have seriously shaken that view, however. Anthropologist David Meltzer, quoted earlier, wonders how a relatively thin population of foragers could do that much damage all by themselves, especially since they needed hard-to-find chalcedony, chert, and other crystalline stone to make their spear points. Bands of hunters moving quickly through mountains, plains, and forests would scarcely have time to find the necessary raw materials for their weapons. "It is now clear," writes Meltzer, "that Paleoindians hunting was not the prime cause of, and, perhaps, did not even contribute to the terminal Pleistocene extinctions." The more likely explanation for the extinctions is the relatively rapid climate change that followed on the retreat of the glacial ice sheets, a change too rapid for some of the mammals, especially the larger ones, to contend with. And so a more likely scenario may be that, while some of the early bands of Indians kept moving, drifting down into Central and South America, there were others that clearly preferred to stay put in North America, once they found a suitable place to settle. One of the most suitable turned out to be a fertile, game-filled valley in the northeast corner of what is now Alabama. Here, at the base of a low mountain at the western side of the valley, is a large cave-shelter that was so useful and agreeable that it was occupied on a seasonal basis (fall and winter), if not year-round, by Indian families for some 9,000 years. The place is now preserved as **Russell Cave National Monument**.

The most recent archaeological materials recovered from the site show the use of the cave as a hunting camp by Indians as late as the early 1600s. The earliest reliably dated evidence of human habitation found *in* the cave (the remains of a campfire) are Early Archaic, a period coming immediately after that of the Paleo-Indians. In 1993, a visiting archaeologist inspecting

Located in the Tennessee River valley in northeast Alabama, Russell Cave, now a National Monument, holds artifacts from more than 9,000 years of human history in America. During excavations sponsored by the Smithsonian and National Geographic in the 1950s, archaeologist Carl F. Miller (lower left) discovered implements 23 feet below the cave's floor that carbon-14 analysis dated to the Early Archaic period.

an eroded area near the cave where rainwater had washed away the earth leaned over and pulled what looked very much like a Clovis point from beneath some rocks. "We suspected that Russell Cave was a Paleo site," says Farrell Saunders, the monument superintendent, "but we basically didn't have anything to prove it." As it turned out, the spear point was a "transitional" type, not quite Clovis, but definitely predating the plainer Archaic style. It was, says Saunders, the greatest good fortune that this crucial find had not been pocketed by a visitor.

Thus, the astonishing fact is that occupation of this single cave covers almost the entire span of human habitation in America, from Paleo to present.

In the Eastern United States, the main archaeological periods are dated roughly as follows:

Paleo-Indian 11,000 to 9,000 years B.P.
Early Archaic 9,000 to 7,000 years B.P.
Middle Archaic 7,000 to 5,500 years B.P.
Late Archaic 5,500 to 3,000 years B.P.
Woodland 3,000 to 1,500 years B.P.
Mississippian 1,500 to 500 years B.P.
Recent 500 years B.P. to present

Why was Russell Cave so attractive across all these periods? The answer is that this cave was not just a hole in the side of a hill, but a snug yet ample wintertime shelter with, in effect, indoor plumbing and air conditioning. Measuring 107 feet across and 26 feet high, the cave faces eastward, toward the warming morning sun. The air flowing out of the mouth of the cave is a consistent 58 degrees F, providing for summertime comfort and moderating freezing temperatures in winter. As for the plumbing, this was the result of a geological accident that even relatively modern Indians could scarcely improve upon.

The accident had to do with the collapse of the front part of the original cave, a limestone cavern much like other caverns that have been forming and collapsing in these mountains for millions of years. As the slightly acidic rainwater dissolves the limestone strata laid down when this area was covered by the sea, caverns are created. A small stream ran *into* this cave (and still does, emerging from the mountainside two miles away), filling the whole opening. Then, about 10,000 years ago, the roof fell in at the front of the cavern, revealing that behind it was actually a split-level cave with one side high and dry and the other, partially separated from it by a column of rock, running with year-round fresh water that could not freeze over—an important consideration in the early days when the climate was much colder than it is today in northern Alabama. As the years passed, more rock falls occurred. Moreover, flood waters occasionally entered the higher part of the cave, and were trapped behind what amounted to a rock dam. As a result of these two actions—rock falls and layers of sedimentation from flooding (and perhaps the deliberate addition of soil by humans to cover campfires and burial places)—the floor of the cave rose in layers, each containing artifacts and other evidence of the people occupying it. Thus, after many thousands of years, the original bottom of the cave now lies 30 feet below the present surface, permitting the cultural development of the Indians—Archaic, Woodland, Mississippian—to be read in cross section.

The archaeological value of the cave was discovered relatively recently, in 1953, by the Archaeological Society of Tennessee. In that year, the pre-

For thousands of years until as late as the early 1600s, roving Indian families took shelter in Russell Cave, which features a consistent temperature of 58 degrees F and a freshwater stream.

liminary excavations made by the Tennesseans, an amateur group, revealed that the site was of great antiquity and quite complex. Accordingly, they called on the Bureau of American Ethnology of the Smithsonian Institution for professional help. The Smithsonian, unable to secure government funding for professional excavation, turned to the National Geographic Society for financial aid, which was granted. As a result of the first season's work in 1956 by Smithsonian scientists, during which the 9,000 year B.P. date was established by carbon-14 analysis of material uncovered from an ancient hearth, the society decided to buy the farm on which the cave was located (owned by Oscar Ridley; the cave had been named for an earlier settler). Thus secured, excavations could continue without interference. In 1958, the society donated the property to the federal government, and, in 1962, President John F. Kennedy declared the site a national monument and transferred it to the National Park Service. In 1967, the museum at Russell Cave National Monument was formally dedicated.

Excavations in the cave by the Smithsonian, the National Geographic Society, and later the National Park Service revealed seven distinct layers of material containing evidence of human use. Besides the bits of campfire charcoal that determined the earliest date of habitation in the cave, the archaeologists also found clay impressions of cane matting at the lowest level (G), indicating that Early Archaic people knew how to weave plant fibers. Also at this level they found a bone fishhook; bone awls and needles, suggesting leather work; a "flaker" made of a deer antler used to knap projectile points; knives and scrapers; bone and antler ornaments; and stone mortars and mullers. Many points used in hunting have been found at this layer, along with the bones of the animals hunted. One of these includes a species of peccary that is now extinct. Its teeth were found at the bottom of layer G. For the most part, however, deer supplied meat for the diet. One human burial site—that of an infant—was found.

Five more burial sites were located in layer F, the deposits laid down during the Middle Archaic period. Spear points were found throughout all the Archaic layers, but smaller points, indicating the use of bows and arrows, a new invention, appear only at the Early Woodland period, in layers E and D. Also appearing at this time are the first pottery vessels. The abrupt shift in artifacts may be attributed to the intrusion of new people into the area.

At the topmost layer, A, a lone iron fishhook was found, which could have been left there any time between A.D. 1540 and 1800.

Visitors are few at Russell Cave, perhaps because you must drive many miles along country roads to get there (although a new four-lane highway is now being built), and, once arrived, you do not gasp at the view, as at the Grand Canyon. But it is hard to overstate the significance of Russell Cave to our understanding of how the earliest humans lived in America. And the park rangers help bring this history alive. Larry Beane, the park's interpretive archaeologist, is locally famous for his ability to knap arrowheads, which he does perhaps as well as the best of the Archaic hunters. He and his colleagues can demonstrate the *at-latl*, a throwing stick that the Indians used to launch their spears, giving the weapons more leverage and force. They can start a fire with a bow-drill and grind seeds, and they have established a garden much like those planted by the Indians during the spring and summer when they were camping in the valley.

For the park's annual "Indian Days" celebration, volunteers demonstrate the survival crafts and tell the stories of the people. Then, at night, special programs are given in the cave by local Indians performing native music. "It makes you feel as if you were there thousands of years ago," says Farrell Saunders. But even without the costumes and the moonlight and the beating drums, a visitor can stand at the cave mouth, looking outward into Alabama woodlands that are still much the same as in the old days, and, with a bit of imagination, glance back into the cave and envision one of the first human families on this continent, flaking spear points, roasting deer meat over a fire, weaving mats. Such a glance would span 9,000 years in time, yet only a few yards of cave floor, beneath which is the longest continuous record of human culture and heritage we know of.

Indian culture and heritage reached its high point in the Eastern United States along the Scioto River in southern Ohio. Here the remarkable Hopewell people arose, a mound-building civilization of the Woodland period whose reach extended southward to the Gulf of Mexico, eastward to the crest of the Appalachians, northward into what is now Canada, and westward to the Great Plains. This was, during its heyday, the Athens of the pre-Columbian civilization east of the Rockies.

Indian mounds in the United States, only a few of which predate the Hopewells (so named after the owner of land where early excavations took place), can be conical and linear; take the form of serpents, birds, mammals, and people (the so-called effigy mounds), be built like platforms that resemble flat-topped pyramids; and consist of elaborate earthworks. This last type is a form closely associated with the Hopewell culture, although the Hopewells also built conical mounds, some of them for burials. Archaeologists estimate that at one time 200,000 mounds could be found in the Eastern United States. Today, all but a few have been plowed under or have eroded away. The purposes of the mounds are not wholly understood, but the Hopewells' burial mounds, which, by scientific examination of their "grave goods," can give us a clue about the culture that built them. It is only a clue, however, since there is no written language to analyze, and no oral history has survived.

Thus, much of Hopewell culture remains altogether a mystery. It arose in 2200 B.P., lasted for 700 years, and then simply disappeared at 1500 B.P., or A.D. 550. None of the Shawnees, the Delawares, or the Miami Indians who, among other tribes, later inhabited the Hopewell area, had any legends whatsoever about the mounds or the people who built them. They were, at least some experts believe, of a different physical type. The Hopewells had distinctively long heads, quite unlike the rounder heads of other peoples in the area. Moreover, they were most obviously affluent—indeed, the Hopewells went in for conspicuous consumption in a way unknown in any other pre-Columbian people in North America. Had this cul-

Peoples of the Hopewell culture built
thousands of complex mounds, whose
exact purposes remain shrouded in
mystery. Conical mounds, such as those
pictured here, often honored the dead,
who were laid to rest with exquisite
costumes, jewelry, artworks, and ceramics.
The two illustrations above, from an
1848 Smithsonian report, are of sites that
today are buried beneath Marietta, Ohio,
not far from Hopewell Culture National
Historical Park.

ture survived, it might very well have rivaled that of the Aztecs of Montezuma, which peaked a thousand years after that of the Hopewells.

One of the richest collections of Hopewell mounds is in the Mound City unit of **Hopewell Culture National Historical Park**, near Chillecothe, Ohio. The unit contains 23 burial mounds on 13 acres surrounded by an earthen embankment. Within the burial sites, archaeologists have found artworks of exquisite refinement, as well as jewelry, costumes, pottery, and much else. One of the most interesting categories of grave goods buried with the Hopewells' honored dead consists of small ceramic pipes—possibly for smoking, although their use is still not clear—elegantly fashioned into the shapes of birds, mammals, serpents, and people. Ceremonial cups were carved from conch shells. Volcanic glass was fashioned into knives and other instruments. Earrings and beads were shaped from silver and copper, as were breastplates and other finery. Freshwater pearls were used for adornment, and appear to have been a sign of wealth. One grave site, located in a mound area not far from Mound City (there are five units in place or planned as part of the park), contained enough pearls to be worth perhaps

An artist imagines a cremation ceremony of a people of the Hopewell culture, which arose about 2,200 years ago in southern Ohio. Hopewell influence extended southward to the Gulf of Mexico, eastward to the Appalachians, northward into what is now Canada, and westward to the Great Plains.

as much as $5 million in today's dollars. Taken together, the burials in this area, the Hopewell Mound Group, have yielded more than 100,000 pearls.

Mica was favored as a material from which semi-abstract shapes would be formed, with the workmanship and design so sophisticated that many experts theorize the Hopewell culture had sufficient leisure to support a class of professional artists. Ethnologists believe that so rich in food resources and good soils was the Scioto-Ohio River valley region that the Hopewells needed to spend no more than 20 hours a week gathering food and hunting game to provide a rich and healthful diet. Such an Eden-like subsistence could easily create sufficient time for the development of the arts. It is a pity that no written language was developed as well to record the qualities of mind and heart of these remarkable people.

The culture's sufficiency of free time also allowed for the development of what some have called the Hopewell "empire." Yet this was not an empire taken by conquest, but rather by trade, after the manner of the Phoenicians in the Mediterranean. At its peak, the vigorous entrepreneurial hegemony of the Hopewells reached to the Appalachians of the Carolinas (whence came the mica), to the northern Rockies (the obsidian), to Canada (copper and silver), and to the Gulf of Mexico (conch shells)—with artifacts fashioned from all these treasures found in the mounds. The freshwater pearls were collected throughout the Ohio and Mississippi River drainages. Writes Robert Silverberg, an expert on Native American cultures, "To wrap a corpse from head to foot in pearls, to weigh it down in many pounds of copper, to surround it with masterpieces of sculpture and pottery, and to bury everything under tons of earth—this is the kind of wastefulness that only an amazingly energetic culture would indulge in."

Because of such abundant evidence of a high civilization—including remnant parallel embankments (presumably indicating roads) connecting earthwork sites with outlying villages, possibly as far as 60 miles away—a good many early scholars and others interested in the Hopewell culture advanced the theory that these people were not Indians at all. They must have been, went one late-18th-century theory, the Vikings, who also used burial mounds in their native Scandinavia. It was further asserted that these Vikings decamped from Ohio, and became the Toltecs of Mexico. Some, including the president of Yale University at that time, proposed that the Hopewells were descended from the lost tribes of Israel. And yet others wanted them to be the people of Atlantis, or Greeks, or Persians, or Hindus, or (more recently) ancient astronauts. Certainly, the theory went, they could not be related to the relatively uncouth "savages" that the Europeans encountered in the Ohio countryside. There were more responsible views, to be sure, including that of Thomas Jefferson, who did not doubt that the Hopewells were Indians, although not the same Indians as the Shawnees.

Greater questions remain, however. What happened to the Hopewells? Why did their civilization collapse? Where did they go? And, indeed, why did these people engage in mound building and earth moving at this scale to begin with? As Robert Peterson, park ranger and chief interpreter at Hopewell, puts it, "Using clamshells, wooden digging sticks, stone hoes, and baskets, the Hopewell created not just Mound City but dozens of enclosures,

Peoples of the Hopewell culture sometimes traveled great distances in search of materials to craft into elaborate burial items. Incised with a stylized human hand, the stone disk, above, was unearthed in a Hopewell burial mound, as was this the reel-shaped gorget, or neck ornament, below, fashioned from copper collected in the Great Lakes area and found in the Naples mound, Illinois.

Located in New Mexico's remote Chaco Canyon, Pueblo Bonito, opposite, is the largest of the Anasazi Great Houses. Occupied from about A.D. 900 to 1250, Pueblo Bonito contained more than 600 rooms and rose at least four stories. It is now part of the Chaco Culture National Historical Park.

moving thousands of tons of earth. Even by today's standards, the earthworks created by these people challenge the imagination."

But, for some reason, they gave up these practices. After about A.D. 500, no mounds were built for several hundred years. By about A.D. 1000, other cultures resumed mound building in the Middle West and the South, although not for burial in the same way as the Hopewells. The Hopewells' earthworks perhaps served as models for later people, but no one was to match their obsessive creativity and display ever again.

Archaeology provides few if any clues to the cause of the Hopewell diaspora, if that is what it was—no indications of genocidal war or a devastating epidemic or a natural disaster. One possibility, advanced by Smithsonian archaeologist David Braun, is that the Hopewells eventually became farmers. At first, they could manage quite well on foraging and hunting from their scattered villages, augmented by garden plots. The wide network of trade did, in fact, facilitate such a lifestyle, for the far-flung alliances served as a kind of support group during hard winters, long droughts, or other lean times. But, inevitably perhaps, being clever people, they learned too well how to grow crops and store food. The necessity for trade routes—and the earthworks related to the acquisition and conversion of trade goods to grave goods—simply collapsed. And with them collapsed an elaborate culture based on trade, art, and the worship of the dead. In time, the Hopewells were simply absorbed into neighboring tribes. After many generations, an occasional "long head" would be seen on a newborn child, but its provenance would be a mystery.

Mystery attends the disappearance of another, and quite different, high culture in pre-Columbian North America—that of the Anasazis in the Southwest. The term *Anasazi* was given to these people by the Navahos, the Athabaskans who came later to occupy this region and who still inhabit it—the vast, arid "Four Corners" area, which, by taking in substantial parts of New Mexico, Colorado, Arizona, and Utah, is the size of a Western state itself. Anasazi means "the old enemies," even though by all accounts it was the predatory, nomadic early Navahos who were the enemies of the urban civilization that preceded them.

How advanced this early culture actually became is nowhere so strongly suggested as by the "Great Houses" found in a remote canyon in northwestern New Mexico, near the epicenter of the San Juan River basin (which also describes the Four Corners area). Here, in Chaco Canyon, at the end of a long dirt road, is the **Chaco Culture National Historical Park**, in the view of many the most fascinating prehistoric archaeological site in North America.

Quite recently, archaeologists have come to believe that the Great Houses of the Chacoan people were not houses at all, but, in effect, government buildings serving the vast region of Chacoan influence. The buildings apparently had manifold functions—for religious, administrative, and warehousing purposes. The remains of nine Great Houses are still standing

First Families and Fellow Immigrants

in Chaco Canyon, separated from one other in such a way that this appears to be a planned city, as is Washington, D.C., for example, or Brasília. Like medieval cathedrals, which took many centuries to build, the Great Houses were under construction, or reconstruction, between A.D. 900 and 1115. The largest of the structures, called Pueblo Bonito, had 650 rooms, and, in certain sections, rose five stories in height. The walls are made of thin sandstone slabs, mortared with exquisite care in intricate masonry patterns of various kinds, depending on the type of sandstone used. Inside, the walls were plastered and whitewashed with a gypsum coating.

Pueblo Bonito is D-shaped, with the curved part of the structure containing rooms formed around a large, central plaza studded with kivas—round, subterranean chambers used for religious ceremonies. That the rooms of the pueblo, organized as suites, were not apartments (an early archaeologist once described Pueblo Bonito as the largest apartment house in the United States until 1885, when a larger one was built in New York City) is deduced from the lack of hearths or any other evidence of fires for heat, light, or cooking. Moreover, according to archaeologists Stephen H. Lek-

Working without metal tools, the Anasazis of Chaco Canyon constructed about 40 large, round, subterranean chambers called kivas, opposite and below, in Pueblo Bonito, which they may have used for communal gatherings and rituals.

Symbols used in Pueblo Bonito petroglyphs suggest that the sun, moon, and stars played a significant role in the lives of the Chaco Anasazi. Their kindred in the Four Corners region—the juncture of present-day Utah, Colorado, Arizona, and New Mexico—constructed the pueblo, opposite, that nestles in the mighty canyons of Canyon de Chelly National Monument, Arizona.

son, Thomas C. Windes, John R. Stein, and W. James Judge, the suites were not accessible from inside the house. "If the Great Houses were primarily for habitation," they write, "one would expect storage rooms to be accessible to their inhabitants. The existence of doors that open only to the exterior of the building implies instead that the suites are road-related storage rooms of some kind." It is likely that administrators and priests, rather than large numbers of ordinary people, lived in parts of these giant structures.

Although the roads to which Lekson and his colleagues refer are difficult for the casual visitor to see, they are no less amazing than the Great Houses, and suggest a high degree of centralized government, based at Chaco. The roads are straight, graded, of consistent width (30 feet), and long—a network reaching out from the center (like the avenues in Washington, D.C.) that extended hundreds of miles from the canyon as if engineered for wheeled traffic. And yet these were a people who, like the Aztecs, did not use wheels!

Another mysterious feature of Chaco Canyon is the Fajada Butte solstice marker. The butte contains three large sandstone slabs that are positioned in front of rock carvings incised into one of the butte's vertical rock faces. One of the designs is a spiral, upon which, when the sun is in the proper position,

a "dagger" of light appears, indicating seasonal changes. At the summer solstice, the dagger bisects the center of the spiral; at the winter solstice, it lies along the spiral's edge. The phenomenon was discovered in 1977 by artist Anna Sophaer, who has proposed that the Fajada spiral, with its sun dagger, attests to great astronomical sophistication. Others are not sure of the design's full meaning, but most agree that the site played an important role in Chacoan life and worship during the days of the Great Houses.

Around A.D. 1250, the Chacoans abandoned the Great Houses they had built in the canyon and elsewhere throughout the San Juan River basin-Four

Above, an ancient kiva at Mesa Verde National Park, Colorado. The first Mesa Verde Anasazis settled here about A.D. 550 and are known as Basketmakers for their skill at that craft. The cliff dwellings at right are located in the Keet Seel ruins of Navajo National Monument, Arizona.

Corners area. The causes are undoubtedly complex. One of the reasons most often cited concerns a prolonged drought in the region. That this was the sole cause of the abandonment seems unlikely, however, since there never was much water at Chaco Canyon. Possibly the drought came at a time of general administrative weakness in the elaborate system of food storage and ritual at the Great Houses. Says National Park Service archaeologist Dabney Ford, "The bureaucrats running the place were controlling populations, the distribution of food, and directing the building of these monuments. Their payback—the benefit to the people for these controls—was harmony. When that doesn't happen, what do you do? You get rid of the bureaucrats. Or you just don't pay attention to them any more."

No one knows, of course, exactly what happened or exactly why. The park service's Ford says that she and her archaeological colleagues recently have begun to deconstruct the Navahos' ancient legends and rituals, which may contain significant clues about the people they replaced in the high desert country of the Southwest. But so far we know only that the Anasazi culture collapsed and the people dispersed. Their descendants, who have continued the urban tradition of the Chacoans, though in a less spectacular

Analysis of samples taken from ancient timbers reveals that the Kayenta Anasazis—the third Anasazi cultural division, along with the Chaco and Mesa Verde—built the cliff dwellings, opposite, about A.D. 1275. They are now part of Navajo National Monument, Arizona. Above, sunrise over a Spanish mission and pueblo ruins at Salinas Pueblo Missions National Monument, New Mexico.

The ruins of Pecos pueblo and a Spanish mission, top, Pecos National Historical Park, New Mexico. The kiva (foreground) was a special religious place for the Pecos, thought to be located between the underworld, where the Indians believed they originated, and the world above. The Pecos enjoyed a rich cultural tradition, exemplified by beautiful crafts, above.

way, may be found in the present-day Indian pueblos of New Mexico and Arizona, some of which, such as Taos, predate the time of the abandonment of the Great Houses.

Just a few hundred years after the Anasazis drifted away from Chaco Canyon, a European, Christopher Columbus, in the name of the Spanish Crown, made a landfall in the Bahamas. Unlike the aborted efforts of the Norse people to populate the Labrador coast in A.D. 1000, Columbus's arrival would initiate what would later be called the "Atlantic migration," with increasing numbers of Europeans arriving in the New World. The Norse, with arms scarcely if at all superior to those of native populations, were persuaded to give up their dreams of settlement. But the Spaniards had powerful ordnance—muskets and cannons—plus one more weapon: a missionary zeal to convert the natives to the doctrines of Christianity. There are impressive reminders throughout the Southeast and Southwest United States of just how consequential Spanish gunpowder and the Catholic Church have been to our history. The soldiers and clergy of Spain had, after all, a one-century advantage over competing nations—England and France—to extend their military and spiritual domain in North America.

Having established a solid beachhead in the West Indies during the first decade of the 16th century, Spain sought to consolidate its new empire in Central and South America, and then headed north to new lands where the

A portion of a colorful Navajo drawing depicts one of the many Spanish Christian missionary groups that arrived at Canyon de Chelly. The drawing was found in Canyon del Muerto, or "Massacre Cave," named for a fierce, day-long battle against the Spanish in 1805 in which 115 Navajos were killed.

natives were not yet subdued. The initial points of entry in what was to become the continental United States were two: the coast of Florida, which had been discovered by Ponce de Leon in 1513; and the American Southwest, where, in 1540, Coronado moved his columns, with the Jesuits and Franciscans following afterward. Two national historic treasures, one representing conquest and empire, the other the power of the church, offer compelling illustrations of just how powerful, and lasting, the Spaniards' influence in North America has been. They are Castillo de San Marcos in Florida and the Tumacacori Mission church in Arizona.

One of the most interesting aspects of the history of the first of these places, the **Castillo de San Marcos National Monument**, is not how long ago this amazing fort was built but how recently, relative to the establishment of the Spanish empire in the New World. Located in northern Florida, the castillo was not begun until 1672, almost two centuries after Columbus arrived, and the fort remained in Spanish hands for the next century, playing a key role in the struggle between Spain, France, and England for dominance in North America. That England won this struggle is not news, of course, but that Spain held sway for so long is, at least for many non-Floridians, something of a revelation.

Castillo de San Marcos served as the northernmost outpost of Spain's American empire, guarding trade routes from Central America and the Caribbean to Spanish ports. It was the Gulf Stream, whose navigational importance was first understood by Ponce de Leon, that determined the location of the fort. This northeasterly flowing tropical current provided a speedy route for the Spanish ships to carry the plunder of gold and silver from Mexico and Peru to Cádiz. Running north from the Caribbean along the coast of Florida, the Gulf Stream keeps close to shore. Accordingly, Spanish control of the southern coast was of extraordinary strategic importance. Otherwise, the swift French corsairs and the English privateers and pirates, holed up in coastal anchorages along the route, could easily pounce on the heavy Spanish galleons laden with booty.

Moreover, the English had begun settling in areas not far north of Florida—notably in Virginia and the Carolinas. With the Spanish Armada defeated, in 1588, the English could, and did, devote increased energy to colonizing America, and presumably would be moving southward. The Spanish had put off building a major fort to protect Florida from the north, but after repeated attacks on the city of St. Augustine, founded in 1565, the Spanish military gradually became aware that they could easily lose their toehold in North America should Florida fall. After many wooden forts at St. Augustine had been destroyed one after another for more than a century, culminating in the sack of St. Augustine in 1668 by English pirates, the Spanish finally became convinced that a major north-Florida fortress was called for, and should be as nearly impregnable and as daunting to the enemies of Spain as possible. So began the construction of what would be the most impressive masonry fort erected anywhere in the continental United States.

The key to the fort's impregnability turned out to be a rare, extremely soft and porous marine-shell conglomerate called *coquina*, taken from damp, shallow quarries on Anastasia Island, just a quarter of a mile away from the site. When wet, the stone was easy to cut and shape, but once exposed to the air for a time it hardened and became durable and strong. The coquina-block walls of the castillo were built 14 feet to 19 feet thick at the base, narrowing to between 9 feet and 11 feet thick at the top. The fort, like most European forts of the period, was square, with a courtyard within and bastions jutting out from each corner. Those at the castillo were diamond-shaped, an innovation that provided a means for close-range crossfire from the parapets and reduced the ability of enemies to scale the outer walls.

The Spanish mounted their cannons, each weighing 6,000 pounds, on the top of the parapets, and conducted gunnery training often, using a sandbar across the bay from the fort as a target. During one attack on the fort, the English, ignorant of this practice, set up a line of cannon on the bar. Amazed at how easily the Spaniards got their range, they quickly withdrew.

Thanks to the special properties of coquina, the fort could, in any event, withstand extremely heavy cannon fire, as well as deliver it. The enemy balls would simply dent the stone, which absorbed the energy like a pillow, so that the castillo walls could retain their strength and integrity without cracking or crumbling as might stone with a crystalline structure. In 1702, when the fort was under heavy bombardment from the English during a 50-day siege, the Spanish would slip out at night (or so the legend has it) and whitewash the walls so that from a distance the enemy was led to believe that its cannon-fire had missed entirely. While the city of St. Augustine fell to the ene-

my, the fort held. In fact, throughout its long history, Castillo de San Marcos has never been taken in battle.

The fort was transferred to the British in 1762, when Spain ceded Florida to Great Britain. Then, in a 1784 settlement of territory after the Revolutionary War (during which Florida remained on the Loyalist side), the fort was returned to Spain. But by that time, the strategic importance of Florida was much diminished, and Spain was, in any event, preoccupied with rebellions throughout its South American possessions. In 1821, Florida, and Castillo de San Marcos with it, was ceded at last to the United States.

The grand old castillo was immediately renamed Fort Marion, and, during the Seminole wars, was used mainly as a prison. By the outbreak of the Civil War, it was abandoned, and, when the Confederate army sought to take it over, all they found was one lone Union soldier serving as caretaker. He gladly gave up the keys to the place and went home, but not before demanding—and receiving—a signed receipt from the Confederates.

In 1924, the fort, by then a recognized historic site, was proclaimed a national monument and given to the War Department for administration. In 1933, it was transferred to the National Park Service, and, in 1942, the fort's original name, Castillo de San Marcos, was restored. Today, while an American flag flies above monument headquarters nearby, the flag of Old Spain flies over the castillo, in recognition of the importance of Spanish heritage in Florida. On summer weekends, "reenactors," volunteers who "dress out" in period uniforms and costumes, greet visitors and help fire off the cannons.

The Spanish built Castillo de San Marcos between 1672 and 1695 to protect St. Augustine, in what is today Florida, from pirates and the British.

The two Spanish conquistadors most intimately associated with Florida are Ponce de Leon, who discovered the peninsula for the Europeans in the first

place, and Hernando de Soto, who arrived in 1539 and led a bloody foray north into what are now most of the Southern states in search of gold, silver, and jewels, killing any Indians who might have objected. Yet another of these astonishing Florida explorers was the one-eyed, grizzled veteran, Pánfilo de Narváez, who mounted an expedition that landed a few years before de Soto, in 1528. Narváez's effort was a disaster, but it set off a strange concatenation of events that led ultimately to the Spanish exploration, conquest, and subsequent Christianization of the American Southwest two thousand miles away.

Here is how it happened. Narváez's expedition, 300 strong, came ashore near the present-day city of Tallahassee. But after traveling only a few hundred miles inland they were so beset by hostile Indians that they retreated to the landing point to await a resupply ship. They waited in vain. Near starvation, the company built crude boats and set off across the Gulf of Mexico toward the safety of the settled Spanish port of Veracruz, from which they could easily travel overland to Mexico City.

The plan didn't work out. A violent storm arose, driving the frail boats toward shore, where they broke up in the heavy surf on an island off the Texas coast. All hands were lost save five—a young nobleman named Cabeza de Vaca (cow's head), three other Spaniards, and a black man named Estevanico. The small band made their way onto the Texas mainland, wandered west into New Mexico and Arizona, and, some believe, even reached California before heading south toward Mexico City, a journey that took seven years and covered 3,000 miles of Southwest American landscape! Of the five, only one man succumbed during the arduous trek. But Estevanico made it, as did Cabeza de Vaca. (The nobleman's name is a common one in New Mexico, where for the most part it has been corrupted to de Baca or just Baca, and, curiously, C de Baca, with no period after the initial.)

When the four survivors arrived in Mexico City in 1536, what marvelous tales they had to tell: of giant "hunchbacked" cows, for they were the first white men to see buffalo; of the Indians whose arrowheads were made of gemstones; and of the rich pueblos where the people lived in peace and harmony. Based on their accounts, the viceroy of New Galicia, with dreams of gold, silver, and jewels, got Estevanico to guide a Franciscan friar named Marcos de Niza into the territory to the north, now Arizona and New Mexico, to determine where the great riches might be located. Eager to be the bearer of good news when he returned (the brave Estavanico had been killed), Fray Marcos told the viceroy that, while he and Estavanico did not find anything themselves, they had learned from the Indians (probably the Zunis) of the "Seven Cities of Cibola," whose streets were paved with turquoise and whose people ornamented themselves with gold from head to foot. The viceroy immediately appointed a brash young captain named

Now a National Monument, the Castillo de San Marcos is the oldest masonry fort in the continental United States. Its baptism of fire came in 1702, when the English unsuccessfully besieged the fort for 50 days.

Francisco Vasquéz de Coronado to head an expedition to find these cities of gold and bring back the treasure. The year was 1540.

No gold was found, of course. Coronado returned empty-handed after four years of searching throughout Arizona, New Mexico, the Texas panhandle, even into Oklahoma and Kansas. Yet the various expeditions by Coronado and his lieutenants were of great historical significance, for following upon these military forays came the Spanish missionaries, whose powerful influence on the Indians over the next several centuries was a defining one for the American Southwest.

The most beloved of these missionaries (and not all were, by any means) was in fact from the north of Italy, though in service to the Jesuits of New Galicia: Father Eusebio Francisco Kino. Kino, following the early route of Coronado up through Sonora and into southern Arizona, a region called *La Pimería Alta*, established a string of missions that predated the more famous mission system in Alta California of Father Junípero Serra.

The first Spanish mission in what is now Arizona was established by Kino in 1691 at Tumacacori, about 20 miles north of Nogales. Here, the ruins of a magnificent church built a century later by the local Pima Indians serves as the centerpiece of the **Tumacacori National Historical Park**. Just as Castillo de San Marcos expresses the great military power of Spain, so in Tumacacori the Spanish mission demonstrates the ecclesiastical power of the Catholic Church. While the military presence faded and disappeared from North

The centerpiece of Tumacacori National Historical Park, ruins of a Catholic church, above and right, lie near the site where in 1691 Father Eusebio Francisco Kino established the first Spanish Catholic mission in what is today Arizona. Pima Indians finished construction of this church in 1822, more than a century after Kino had died.

First Families and Fellow Immigrants

America, the dominion of the church has continued for centuries. Much of the reason for this dominion in the Southwest was the ministry of Father Kino, who is still revered today in southern Arizona and northern Sonora as a kind of combination Daniel Boone, Thomas Jefferson, and St. Paul.

Like many Jesuits of his time (and ours), Father Kino was superbly educated, having attended some of the great universities of Europe. He joined the Jesuit order after surviving a deadly illness as a youth. He promised God that if he were allowed to live he would devote his life to the church. Hoping for a missionary assignment to China, Kino was nevertheless assigned to New Galicia, where he led expeditions to Baja California and later across the Spanish frontier to the north into the Pimería Alta region, a vast territory straddling what is now the Mexico-U.S. border, where no white man had been seen since the days of Coronado.

Kino, like Jefferson, had a knack for scientific agriculture, and taught the Indians he encountered new ways to grow crops. He was, like Daniel Boone, a fearless explorer of the wilderness, mapping the regions he served. And, like St. Paul, he brought a new religion to the varied peoples of a large geographical area. His missionary zeal was tempered, however, by a sincere regard for the Indians' indigenous religion and a generous interest in their temporal welfare. As a result, he succeeded where more narrowly orthodox

Mission San José, opposite, is one of four Spanish missions preserved in San Antonio Missions National Historical Park, Texas. Fray Antonio Margil de Jesús, a Franciscan, founded San José in 1720, two years after the creation of Mission San Antonio de Valero, below, commonly known as the Alamo and now a Texas State Historic site. Both buildings portray the influence of Spanish architecture on the Southwestern frontier.

missionaries failed. Everywhere Father Kino went in his circuit rides of baptism and preaching among the Indians, he was greeted by arches of flowers and large wooden crosses.

Father Eusebio Kino died in 1711, long before the great church was built at Tumacacori near the site where he had held his first services in a crude ramada. Indeed, it was perhaps a mercy that he died when he did, for he was thereby spared expulsion from New Galicia. Fearing that the Jesuits were disloyal to the crown, Carlos III of Spain ordered the "Black Robes," as they were called, rounded up and sent home, to be replaced by the presumably more loyal, gray-cassocked Franciscans. As a result, with Kino gone and his colleagues expelled, a long period of inaction ensued on the northern Pimería frontier.

Finally, a Franciscan friar, Narciso Gutíerrez, was able to begin construction of a permanent church, which, after many travails—Apache raids, the Mexican Revolution, and Father Gutíerrez's own death—finally was completed, at least enough for use, in 1822, more than a century after Father Kino was laid to rest. With its tall, plastered walls, its 75-foot nave, its barrel vaults and impressive dome, the mission church was, and still is, a startling edifice to find in the midst of the lightly populated Santa Clara River valley, where the great "Padre on Horseback" had taught the Indians about Jesus and about growing corn.

In the end, the church was used for only 26 years after its completion. Located at the very edge of Mexican territory, it was abandoned in 1848 after the conclusion of the Mexican War. Five years later, the Gadsden Purchase placed Tumacacori within the boundaries of the United States, and the structure, already crumbling, became the target for looters and treasure seekers. It had been rumored that the early Jesuits had hidden great hordes of gold within the church, despite the fact that the Jesuits were long gone before the church was built. Utterly ignorant of history and heedless of their desecration, the gold-seekers pulled up the floor and stripped the plaster from the walls in their futile avarice. According to National Park Service historian Don Garate, some people even today ask about the probable location of the secret Jesuit treasure.

At length, the ruined church was rescued by President Theodore Roosevelt, who made it a national monument in 1908. In 1919, work was begun to stabilize the structure, an effort that has continued as funds become available. There are no plans to restore the church to its pre-1848 condition. In 1990, Congress added two related sites several miles distant—one a Kino mission and the other a later Jesuit mission—and renamed the expanded monument Tumacacori National Historical Park.

An annual festival is held at Tumacacori the first weekend in December, with dances and music, arts-and-crafts exhibits, and delicious ethnic foods. Lest the true meaning of the place be overshadowed, however, since 1993, at the instigation of Don Garate, a high mass has been celebrated each spring as an historic reenactment of the remarkable achievements of Father Kino. The officiating priest, the altar servers, members of the congregation, and the orchestra and choir all wear period costumes, as if the Padre on Horseback himself might momentarily arrive. The mass is sung entirely in

Latin. Surely Father Kino would be pleased. Perhaps only arches of flowers and the crude wooden crosses of the Indians he loved and who loved him would make him feel more at home.

For some years, an effort has been underway to canonize Father Kino. All the qualifications for sainthood are proven, save one: no miracle has yet been attributed to him. "But that is wrong," says Don Garate. "This church—this monument to faith—is his miracle. Just look at it." And so we should.

The three principal European powers vying for hegemony in the New World were—in North America—Spain, France, and England. New Amsterdam, the only other European colony on the East Coast, was settled much later, with quite limited territory. In 1664, it fell to the British, who renamed it New York. The only other nation with designs on our part of the hemisphere was Russia, which claimed Alaska during the 18th century and set up trading posts along the Pacific Coast southward to northern California. The Russians made no effort to colonize, however, and, in 1867, the United States purchased Alaska from the Russians for $7.2 million.

Among "the big three," the French claimed the vast interior of the North American continent, fanning out from the Mississippi drainage, but their efforts to establish permanent colonies were quite limited compared with those of England and Spain. The Quebec region was first explored by Jacques Cartier via the St. Lawrence River in the 1530s and '40s, but no settlements were established at that time. Finally, in 1590, Henry IV, the Huguenot king of France, having brought the European "Wars of Religion" to a close, turned his attention to developing a colonial presence in Canada. The first successful French colony in the New World, Quebec, was created in 1608 by Samuel de Champlain.

As for the Spanish, their colonial efforts were, as we have seen, largely confined to the southern regions of North America. Accordingly, with the French to the north and the Spanish to the south, the greater part of the East Coast was open to English settlement. And it was the English, of all the European powers, who had the greatest ambition to create permanent colonies in this part of the New World.

Their first effort to do so ended in a disaster. But it was a disaster of great dramatic impact, surely the most fascinating and mysterious event in British colonial history. And you can stand in the place where it happened. You can see tantalizing clues about it discovered by archaeologists. You can even attend a wonderful pageant that dramatizes the incident based on contemporary accounts. But the true story remains a mystery that perhaps will always elude us—the mystery of the lost colony of Roanoke, the first English settlement in America. The colony is commemorated at **Fort Raleigh National Historic Site** on Roanoke Island, in the Outer Banks region of North Carolina.

The story begins in March 1584. France is embroiled in civil war, the Catholics opposing the Protestant Huguenots. The English have sided with the Huguenots, and much depends on the outcome. Returning from the French wars, a British soldier, courtier, poet, and adventurer named Walter

In 1586, 116 British colonists disappeared forever from the quiet wooded area, above, on what is today Roanoke Island, North Carolina. The colonists were the second group sponsored by Sir Walter Raleigh. A reconstruction of their earthen fort, as seen in this photograph, is now part of Fort Raleigh National Historic Site.

Wind brushes salt-marsh cord grass, above right, at Cedar Island National Wildlife Refuge, located about 75 miles south of Fort Raleigh. Such landscapes are characteristic of the Outer Banks.

Raleigh, a favorite (then) of Queen Elizabeth, is granted a patent entitling him to colonize any lands he might discover in the New World in the name of the Crown. The Old World is in turmoil, with more turmoil to come, for Spain is beginning to build her great armada, with which she hopes to conquer England once and for all. And the New World is up for grabs.

Immediately, the impetuous Raleigh, age 30, commissions two barks, under the command of Philip Amadas and Arthur Barlowe, to sail to North America and scout out the territory. Raleigh does not accompany his men. Amadas and Barlowe arrive at the Outer Banks in July, and claim the area in the name of Queen Elizabeth. The Algonquian Indians the expedition encounters are, as Barlowe is to write later, "gentle, loving, and faithful, void of all guile." By August, the expedition is back in London, and they have brought two Algonquians with them, Wanchese and Manteo, the latter a member of the Croatoan tribe, which lives on an island of the same name near Roanoke. The Indians smoke *uppowoc* (tobacco). They are the toast of the city.

Raleigh is knighted in January 1585, and in April of that year, just 12 months after the first voyage, Sir Walter mounts a second expedition of seven

Sir Walter Raleigh's 1584 expedition to the New World may have first reached North America at a spot similar to this freshwater marsh, left, at Pea Island National Wildlife Refuge in North Carolina's Outer Banks. Historical structures at Jamestown, Virginia, which in 1607 became the first permanent English settlement in the New World, include the excavated foundation of a merchant's row house, top, built in the 1660s, and the Ambler mansion, above, circa 1750.

vessels to the Outer Banks, which he has named "Virginia" after Elizabeth I, the virgin queen. Sir Richard Grenville is placed in command of a company of 500 men, of which 108 are the advance colonists. These include Governor-to-be Ralph Lane, trained as a soldier; John White, the explorer-artist; the famed astronomer-mathematician-writer-surveyor Thomas Harriot; and Joachim Gans, a brilliant Bohemian-Jewish metallurgist. Raleigh remains in London. Manteo and Wanchese return to their home with Grenville.

The object of the second expedition is to conduct a thorough, year-long investigation of the resources, natural history, and indigenous peoples of the area, and to establish a permanent town that can receive colonists to come. After these 108 first colonists are dropped off by Grenville in June 1585, they construct an earthen fort to defend against Spanish attack and build living quarters for themselves of wattle and daub within its embankments. Lane explores the Albemarle Sound and its major tributaries. White makes many paintings of the Indians and the plants, animals, and geographical features roundabout. Harriot studies the fauna and flora. Gans sets up a scientific laboratory to conduct metallurgical studies. It is the first scientific laboratory on the North American continent.

In the spring of 1586, Lane comes to believe that the Indians may be conspiring to kill the colonists, and so leads a preemptive sneak attack on an Indian village where the Indian chief Wingina is killed. It is a bad mistake. Meanwhile, Grenville's resupply ships fail to show up at the appointed time, although, unbeknownst to Lane, they are on the way. On June 10, 1586, Sir Francis Drake puts in at Roanoke after a raid on St. Augustine. He offers to leave a bark to carry everyone back to England. At first the offer is refused; then, after a storm comes up, Lane makes the command decision to abandon the island after all. On June 18, the colonists leave hurriedly, losing many of White's valuable pictures and Harriot's notes in the process. Three men, off on an expedition, are left behind. Three weeks later, Grenville's resupply ships arrive carrying 400 men. The main body of colonists having fled, Grenville decides to leave only a small detachment of 15, and returns to England.

Although disappointed that the advance colonists have returned, Raleigh nevertheless incorporates "The Cittie of Ralegh in Virginia" in January 1586, and in May sends another group of colonists off to Roanoke Island, this time under the command of John White. Raleigh does not accompany them; indeed, he is never to set foot in North America. The three ships of the expedition carry 117 men, women, and children, including White's married daughter, Eleanor Dare. They arrive safely at Roanoke in July, and set about to repair the fort and improve the "cittie." On August 18, Eleanor Dare gives birth to a child, the first born of English colonists on American soil. The girl is named Virginia. Nine days later, her grandfather, John White, as leader of the colony, reluctantly returns to England to secure additional supplies. He arranges with the colonists that, if something should

Split-rail fences line Surrender field at Yorktown, Virginia, site of the last major siege of the American Revolution.

Yorktown, together with Williamsburg and Jamestown, constitutes Colonial National Historical Park, Virginia.

First Families and Fellow Immigrants

A statue of Pocahontas stands in Jamestown, Virginia. The daughter of the powerful intertribal leader Powhatan, Pocahontas became a legend in American folk history for supposedly saving the life of Captain John Smith, founder and leader of the Jamestown colony, after he had been captured by the Indians.

cause them to leave the fort at Roanoke, they should carve their destination on a tree. If they have to leave because of an attack, they are to carve a Maltese cross along with the message.

The trip home is beset with storms, and White does not arrive in London until late October. Quickly he sets about to organize a resupply convoy, but by then the Spanish Armada is on the high seas, bent on totally destroying the hated English. White manages to sail westward with two small ships, but they are attacked by the French and must turn back. Even though the English defeat the Armada decisively, White is unable to organize a new convoy until 1590, three years after leaving Roanoke. He arrives on August 18, his granddaughter Virginia's third birthday. From his ship, he sees smoke from what may be a signal fire. But when he wades ashore he finds there is no fire. The houses have been taken down. His daughter and granddaughter and everyone else are gone. The word "CROATOAN" is carved on a palisade, but not a Maltese cross. Heartsick, White tries to get to Croatoan Island, but foul weather forces the ships to return to England.

End of story. No trace or even the slightest clue to the fate of the colonists was ever found, though many attempts were made over the years. And their fate is still a mystery, the stuff of legend and of the wonderful pageant by playwright Paul Green, "The Lost Colony," which visitors can (and should) attend if they visit Fort Raleigh during the summer.

What is believed to be the remains of one of the 1585–86 Lane fortifications may be seen at the site, as can historical artifacts unearthed by archaeologists, including materials from Gans's laboratory. But the finds have been meager and inconclusive. According to park service historian Alan Smigielski, much of the archaeological evidence may well be under water, since barrier islands, of which Roanoke is one, tend to "move" with the tides. "Possibly," says Smigielski, "the shoreline is now as much as three-quarters of a mile inland, so that the original village site may be out in the sound." Accordingly, despite the difficulties in doing so, archaeologists are now combing the shallows of the bay, hoping that something crucial will turn up.

It is anyone's guess what happened to the lost colony of Roanoke Island; there is little or no consensus among the experts. Some of the colonists may well have set out for Croatoan. Some of them surely died in whatever calamity or ill-fated decision befell them. And some may eventually have intermarried with the Indians, for it has been said by Indians living in the area of the Outer Banks that they have the blood of the lost colonists in their veins. Two of the lost colonists were named Little, which is also the name of the author of this book. Could it be, then, that some of these are cousins?

Despite the failure at Roanoke, the British colonization of America was by any measure wildly successful. And the national park system records this achievement in many places. The first permanent settlement, at Jamestown, is now a part of **Colonial National Historical Park** in Virginia. The site of the Pilgrims' landing in Massachusetts, before they went on to establish Plymouth Colony in 1620, is a part of the **Cape Cod National Seashore**.

Boston, New York, Philadelphia, Baltimore, Richmond, and a number of other Eastern Seaboard cities all contain national park system sites associated with our colonial history.

During the 1600s, the British colonies grew and expanded, and new ones were added during the 1700s until at length there were, as every schoolchild knows, 13 of them. But the British settlers generally clung to the shore, venturing no farther inland than the piedmont of the Appalachians. The first major inland city, Cleveland, was not laid out until 1796, nearly two centuries after Jamestown. It was in 1803 that President Thomas Jefferson commissioned Meriwether Lewis and William Clark to explore the great western reaches of the continent beyond St. Louis (to which we shall return in a later chapter), a fur trading post established by the French in 1763.

At the time of the Lewis and Clark expedition, Jefferson said it would take 40 generations to settle the vast interior of our new continental nation. But, as it turned out, it took only four. Indeed, perhaps the most extraordinary migration event in the United States, at least from the standpoint of the massive amount of land involved, was the settling of the Great Plains. In only a few score years, a billion acres, from Canada to Mexico and from the Appalachians to the Rockies, was converted from a wilderness of prairie grassland to agricultural crops, pasturage, and a skein of settlements that constituted, many believe, the most decent and prosperous small-town agrarian system the world has ever known.

This was Jefferson's dream, but one he would not live to see accomplished. The concept of land for all arose—though perhaps not for the first time—when he was serving as minister to France in 1785. While walking along a mountain path near Fontainebleu, the opulent "hunting lodge" of French royalty, the young diplomat came upon a poor peasant woman who told Jefferson that she was a laborer, the sole support of two children, and earned but eight sous a day when working and none when not, which occurred often. Jefferson gave her 24 sous, ostensibly for serving as his guide, whereupon the poor woman broke into tears of gratitude. His democratic instincts aroused, Jefferson wrote of the incident to his friend Bishop James Madison (cousin to the James Madison who would succeed Jefferson as President), stating, in the now famous lines: "It is not too soon to provide by every possible means that as few as possible shall be without a little portion of land. The small landholders are the most precious part of a state."

Certainly, the new nation had the land for such provision. But the idea of distributing the public estate along the lines prescribed by Jefferson was thwarted in the Congress by Southern members who believed that small parcels of free land would likely be settled by working-class whites disinclined to support Negro slavery. Only after the Southern states left the Union was such legislation possible. "An Act to Secure Homesteads to Actual Settlers on the Public Domain," better known as the Homestead Act, finally was passed and signed into law by President Abraham Lincoln in 1862, long after Jefferson's encounter on the hillside path at Fontainebleu. But the law worked better than even the idealistic Jefferson might have expected. As a result of this act and its successors, 1.7 million American families were provided new farms totaling 147 million acres transferred from the public do-

After the Homestead Act took effect on January 1, 1863, scenes such as the one below on the Santa Fe trail at Great Bend, Kansas, were a common sight in the Midwest, as some 1.7 million American families staked out new farms. Daniel Freeman owned one of the first homesteads, opposite top, near Beatrice, Nebraska. The land Freeman claimed is now the site of Homestead National Monument of America, which features the Palmer-Epard homestead cabin, opposite below, built nearby in 1867.

main to private ownership. In the process, a massive, new migration began, with families moving westward from run-out Eastern farms to the free land on the prairie and with new families arriving from abroad, many of them from Scandinavia. Significantly, it was not necessary to be an American citizen to stake a claim; only a declaration of intent was required.

The Homestead Act provided that any citizen or intended citizen could claim 160 acres, or, in the case of a husband and wife, 320 acres; and if in five years they could show that they were growing crops and had built a permanent dwelling, the land would be theirs, free and clear. The fee was $10 for each quarter section (160 acres) plus a variable commission to the land office depending on whether the land was located inside a railroad-grant area ($8.00) or outside ($4.00). Either way it was a bargain.

The law was to take effect on January 1, 1863. At a New Year's Eve party the night before, in a hotel in Brownsville, Nebraska, a canny young fellow named Daniel Freeman sought out the assistant registrar of the land office located in Brownsville. Freeman told the registrar, whose name was Jami-

son, that he had been ordered to report to St. Louis for duty with the Union Army and had to leave town before the land office opened. But there was some land on Cub Creek near Beatrice, Nebraska, that he had seen and liked. Would it be possible to open the office now? Jamison, doubtless in an agreeable mood, allowed as how it might be, and at about one in the morning on January 1, 1863, Freeman gave him $12, for which he received a receipt for Homestead Application No. 1.

Based on this account, Freeman maintained for the rest of his life (he died in 1908) that he was the first homesteader and that his property should be recognized as the first homestead. Although definitive proof was lacking and other claimants arose—for there were several applications in the land offices around the country during the wee hours of January 1—Freeman's story was accepted as true enough by officials of the U.S. government. As later research revealed, he was not the first "entryman"; at least three others filed

Prairie country at Homestead National Monument of America, Nebraska. At right, the tombstone of Daniel Freeman, who, having staked his claim in Brownsville, Nebraska, at one in the morning on January 1, 1863, proclaimed himself the first homesteader.

DISCOVER AMERICA

earlier in other offices that day. Nor was he the first to "prove" his claim after the requisite five years. By circumstance he was, however, the first of the "first" entrymen in the 30 U.S. land offices to complete all the requirements for full ownership and to receive a patent. His final certificate is dated January 20, 1868.

While it is diverting to delve into who was the first homesteader, this scholarly enterprise should not distract us from the larger issues of the homesteading movement—its extraordinary implications pertaining to the settlement, economy, and ecology of a third of the nation and to the whole history of the United States. It is these issues that today are addressed on the Freeman farm, which is now a unit of the national park system: **Homestead National Monument of America**.

In the view of Constantine Dillon, superintendent at Homestead, the Homestead Act may well have kept the American Dream alive at a time

Amid the tallgrass prairie of Homestead National Monument of America lies the original Freeman homestead site. Before homesteading began, there were vast expanses of tallgrass prairie.

when it might have failed. "When the Industrial Revolution was hitting its peak in the East," says Dillon, "those who were disenfranchised could come out here to get a piece of land."

A sample of what the Easterners encountered in their journey west has been re-created on the acreage of the Freeman farm: the tallgrass prairie. Before homesteading, the tallgrass prairie spread across 400,000 square miles of the Great Plains. "Today less than one percent remains," says Dillon. But even the hundred-acre patch at Homestead is impressive, standing so tall—usually eight feet, and sometimes 10 or 12 feet—that a person could get lost in it. According to Becky Lacome, a park ranger in charge of prairie restoration at Homestead, because of the location of the farm alongside a creek the prairie contains a wide variety of plants, both upland and bottomland species. These include cordgrass, big bluestem, little bluestem, Indian grass, and switch grass, together with lovely perennial flowers—pale purple coneflower, yellow coneflower, black-eyed Susan, Illinois bundleflower, and sunflowers as tall as small trees. To walk *into* this prairie is to understand how exhilarated and terrified the pioneers must have felt, for animals could lurk unseen but five feet from a trail, yet it was a beautiful wild garden nonetheless.

In the museum at Homestead one can find the technological marvel that made farming the plains possible. The instrument was a moldboard plow of a special design called the "prairie breaker." Its plowshare could slice a shallow strip of sod 20 or 30 inches wide, which then the long, low moldboard would turn over in a perfect furrow slice to expose the damp, matted roots of the native grasses underneath. After the first plowing of the virgin sod, the pioneers would chop holes in the turfs with an ax or hatchet, drop a seed in each, then close the holes with their heels. By such means did these "sod-buster" pioneers convert the millions of homestead acres from a climax perennial grassland ecosystem to endless miles of wheat and corn and milo and beans, today farmed by 300-horsepower diesel tractors that can plow a swath of earth 15 feet wide at a speed faster than a person can walk. But there was a price to pay for the destruction of the prairie: the Dust Bowl. Many homesteaders held the belief that "rain follows the plow," and so they pressed ever westward into drier and drier country. They were wrong. When it stopped raining, the earth they had exposed no longer had the roots within it—sometimes extending 15 or 20 feet deep—to hold the soil in place. As a consequence, half the topsoil in the prairie states was washed or blown away. And yet another migration began, this one during the 1930s, from the plowed-out land of the Great Plains westward to California.

Also at Homestead is a pioneer cabin. Though not the one used by the Freeman family, it is typical of the hutlike houses built of logs and lime mortar by the early homesteaders. Where there was no wood available—in areas of little rain—houses, called "soddies," were made of the turfs of grass, sawed into lengths and piled atop one another.

No single site can adequately illustrate the complex story of homesteading in America. The homesteading movement was a unique experiment in land distribution that shaped the politics of the nation forever. It provided Americans with a durable *mythos* having to do with pioneers, the pure country, self-reliance, and the virtues of small towns. It involved perhaps the swiftest and most massive ecosystem disruption by the human hand anywhere in the world. It produced an agricultural technology and economy that no other nation can or ever will match.

"You can trace so much of our history to the Homestead Act," says superintendent Dillon. And surely the best place to start the tracing is at Homestead National Monument of America in Beatrice, Nebraska.

Let us conclude this chapter with the story of one final memorial, this one to an immigration event that, like homesteading, powerfully affected the economic, political, and social structure of contemporary America. It is **Ellis Island National Monument**, perhaps the most emotionally affecting public memorial in the nation.

The monument is meaningful to everyone, of course, for its historic importance is extraordinary. Twelve million immigrants entered through this single portal to America, most of them during a brief 32-year period, from 1892 to 1924. This was the peak, as well as the final phase, of the great "Atlantic migration." But the place itself—its cavernous reception area, its examination rooms, its detention facilities, its dining halls—carries a special resonance for many millions of American families. The significant datum is this: 40 percent of all Americans now living are directly related to someone who immigrated to this country through Ellis Island.

Ellis Island is located in New York harbor, near Liberty Island, with which it is joined administratively by the park service. The Statue of Liberty is itself an important monument to our immigrant history, with its massive size and the affecting lines from Emma Lazarus's sonnet *The New Colossus* inscribed on a plaque:

> Give me your tired, your poor,
> Your huddled masses yearning to breathe free,
> The wretched refuse of your teeming shore.
> Send these, the homeless, tempest-tossed to me,
> I lift my lamp beside the golden door.

One must visit Ellis Island, however, to begin to understand something of the meaning of those lines: how it must have been to be tired and poor, to arrive at last in *America*, and, while yearning to breathe free, have yet to endure the terrifying process of passing inspection by immigration officers. "Do not rub your eyes," says a mother urgently to her crying child. "They won't let you in." The father nods. She was right, for one of the inspections—with a button-hook used to turn back the eyelid—was for trachoma, an incurable infection endemic in Europe that could lead to blindness. If after a hurried examination the child was thought to have trachoma, he would be sent home. Should the mother return with the boy to the *shtetl* and the pogroms, the father to remain in America? Would they ever see each other again?

After being cooped up in cramped steamship steerage quarters for two weeks, the new immigrants, peasant families and tradesmen from Eastern

Millions of new immigrants to the United States have caught a fleeting glimpse of the Statue of Liberty, pictured here in 1938, as they entered New York harbor on their way to Ellis Island.

From 1892 to 1924, some 12 million immigrants passed through this imposing structure—the Main Building of Ellis Island, pictured here in 1905. Forty percent of all living Americans are directly related to someone who entered the United States through Ellis Island, now a National Monument.

and Southern Europe, who had bought passage for $30, must have gasped when tall, domed spires at the corners of the opulent Main Building came into view from the deck of the ferryboat that brought them from the docks of the North River. There were the roof gardens, and the elegant, elaborate masonry of brick and limestone, and the parapets—it seemed like a castle or a cathedral. This *was* the golden door.

But ashore, as they inched up the steps to the registry room in great, long lines, an inspector with a piece of chalk in his hand watched them carefully. Should he see something he didn't like, he would make a mark on the suspect's back or shoulder: an "X" for possible mental deficiency, a "G" for goiter, "L" for a limp, "S" for senility, and the dreaded "CT" for trachoma, against which there was no appeal. In all, there were nearly 20 such marks that meant detention and perhaps deportation.

And then there were the questions: how much money do you have? Right answer: $25. Do you have a contract for a job here? Right answer: no,

After three to five hours of waiting in line and then having to face a lengthy barrage of questions in the registry room of Ellis Island's Main Building, immigrants bound for Manhattan, left, could board a ferryboat, below, that transported them to the city.

The colossal figure of a woman striding across the entrance to New York harbor with uplifted flame is for many a symbol of America. The Statue of Liberty was conceived by Edouard René Lefebvre de Laboulaye, a Frenchman, as an expression of French republican ideals. Completed in 1884, the statue was dismantled and sent to America, where it was dedicated on October 28, 1886.

for the immigration law forbade contract labor. Can you read? Right answer: yes, for reading English was not required. What is your trade? Do you have a relative here? Questions, questions, fired at the exhausted immigrants to see whether they were fit for America.

After the ordeal of registry, the immigrants were confronted by another set of stairs—called the "stairs of separation." The stairway was divided into three by iron banisters. Those who had received their certificate could take the stairs to the left, which led to the ferryboats bound for Manhattan. A third of the immigrants did so. The right-hand stairs led to the railroad ticket offices, where others could arrange for transportation to other cities. But the middle section, to be climbed with an aching heart by those judged needful of further testing, led to the detention area, where some would be rejected outright. About 20 percent of those passing through Ellis Island climbed these middle steps, and often families had to decide in a matter of seconds, standing at the foot of them, whether they would split up or return to Europe together. In the end, approximately 250,000 immigrants were sent back.

But there were tears of joy, too, as families were united. At the "kissing post," where the new immigrants bound for Manhattan met relatives, Katherine Beychok, a Russian Jew coming here in 1910, reports how she saw a striking-looking man walking toward her. "He was so beautiful," she says. "I didn't know he was my father.... Later on I realized why he looked familiar to me. He looked exactly as I did." And so they fell into each other's arms.

These immigrants had come to build America and were glad of it. As Romanian-born poet Andrei Codrescu analyzes the great turn-of-the-century migration, our "ever-growing demand for cheap labor saved millions of people from the no-exit countries of the world. It was a deal that ended up yielding unexpected benefits: vigor, energy, imagination, the remaking of cities, new culture. Restless capital, restless people, ever-expanding boundaries—the freedom to move, pick up, start again, shed the accursed identities of native lands. The deal turned out to have the hidden benefit of liberty."

And yet, we could not quite shed the accursed identities. After the First World War came the "Red Scare" and the hyphenated Americans—the foreign born who might be bomb-throwing anarchists. Emma Goldman, a Jewish-American who had been imprisoned in 1916 for supporting birth control and in 1917 for opposing the draft, was deported to Russia through Ellis Island in 1919. When World War I reduced immigration as much as 90 percent, and it began to surge back after the war, Congress passed an immigration act in 1921 that initiated the idea of quotas. The legislation reduced the flow to half what it had been before the war, but most of the immigrants were dark-skinned, dark-haired Italians and Eastern Europeans. In 1924, Congress passed a new quota law with a "national origins provision" that sought to limit still further the immigration from Mediterranean and Eastern European countries. Although opposition to this law prevented it from going into effect until 1929, it finally made Ellis Island obsolete. It reduced immigration to a trickle compared with the torrent in the early years. Afterwards, though immigrants still arrived, the facilities were used mainly to detain and deport undesirable aliens, particularly during World War II, and as a medical treatment center. By then, the industrial and urban infrastructure of the young

nation had been built; no one else need apply. In 1952, the McCarran-Walter Act, while abolishing the strictly racial quotas of 1924, reaffirmed immigration limits based on national origin. Max Lerner describes the impression given hopeful immigrants by the McCarran-Walter Act: "It was hard for Europeans to fathom a democratic philosophy which admitted only 3,000 French and 5,000 Italians a year, as against roughly 25,000 Germans and 65,000 British."

Thus did the Golden Door swing closed, or almost. And Ellis Island was closed as well, in 1954. But the glory of the nation had passed through its hall of registry and up its stairs of separation. Irving Berlin in 1893. Frank Capra in 1903. Father Flanagan in 1904. Bob Hope in 1908. Hyman Rickover in 1904. Knute Rockne in 1893. A roster of patriots if ever there was one.

Another patriot helped bring Ellis Island back to life—industrialist Lee Iacocca, who headed the Statue of Liberty-Ellis Island Centennial Commission set up in 1982. The island had been declared a national monument by President Lyndon Johnson in 1965, but insufficient funds were available to restore the crumbling buildings. Iacocca, whose own parents were processed through these halls, led the campaign to raise $ 140 million in private funds to rebuild a significant part of Ellis Island, with work completed in 1990. Today Ellis Island is one of the most frequently visited historical sites in the entire national park system. You may take a ferryboat to it from Battery Park in Manhattan or from Liberty State Park in New Jersey. You see the opulent towers. You crowd eagerly down the gangplank, and you climb the very steps that those joyous, terrified immigrants climbed before you. You enter the great hall. Welcome to America.

So have we come to our country, across land and ocean over the span of 12,000 years to populate a continental nation once devoid of humans but now filled with more different kinds of people than any other place on Earth. Our system of national parks tells the story of our arrival literally from the ground up. And one can scarcely imagine a story that can match it, or that is better told.

For many people as potent a symbol of America as the Statue of Liberty, the Golden Gate Bridge spans the entrance to San Francisco Bay, California. About 73,000 acres of land at both ends of the bridge constitute the Golden Gate National Recreation Area.

NATURE'S NATION

The foregoing generations beheld God and nature face to face; we, through their eyes. Why should not we also enjoy an original relation to the universe?…Embosomed for a season in nature, whose floods of life stream around and through us, and invite us by the powers they supply, to action proportioned to nature, why should we grope among the dry bones of the past?

—Ralph Waldo Emerson
Nature

An upstart nation, that's what we were in Europe's eyes after we had won our independence. Uncouth, uncultured, a parvenu. Our history was nil, our art untutored, our literature merely imitative. We had no castles or great monuments or cathedrals or lovely rural landscapes. Accordingly, we tried to find ways wherein we could compare favorably with the Old World.

As it turned out, one of the most wonderful things we did have—and we had it in abundance—took us a nearly a century to understand and appreciate, for at first we feared it: raw nature, untrammeled by the hand of man, unaxed, unplowed, and sometimes even unexplored. But as we surveyed the far reaches of our new nation, we came to understand that the vast and diverse natural areas we discovered were utterly distinctive, unique, extraordinary, phenomenal, superlative. No, they were more than that. Our wilderness vastnesses and sublime landforms were *monuments and cathedrals in themselves*—better, we insisted, than anything pale Europe had to offer. Ours was "nature's nation," said Thomas Jefferson. We now owned a place— this new wilderness—wherein we could, in fact, bear a special relation to nature in a way that in long-settled Europe would be impossible.

As the explorers brought back tales of what they had seen within the vast, empty territory of the United States, the nationalistic view of America's nat-

Minerva Terrace, at Mammoth Hot Springs in Yellowstone National Park, exhibits the bizarre patterns formed by the mineral travertine as it is deposited by the cooling waters of a hot spring. Minerva has been called "a limestone cave turned inside out."

137

ural grandeur slowly but inexorably became an informing influence for the national parks movement. Calls to preserve places of great natural beauty and topographical uniqueness increased during the 1800s as we learned that our incredible natural treasures might be despoiled by our relentless industrial, agricultural, and commercial advance across the continent.

At last—and it was not too late—the statutory protection of these natural areas began in earnest in 1872 with the creation of Yellowstone National Park. As recounted in Chapter 1, additional parks were added slowly at first, but by the turn of the century the pace picked up rapidly, especially as the railroad men and the financiers began to perceive the economic benefits that national park tourism could confer.

The large natural parks that resulted from this joining of patriotic zeal to protect our great natural "cathedrals" and the economic ambition of those who wished to promote tourism produced what are called "the crown jewels" of the national park system. Indeed, a good many Americans tend to think of the park system solely in terms of these well-known tourist destinations—a mistake, as the previous chapters have implied rather strongly. At the same time, just because we are familiar with the Yellowstones and the Yosemites, it would be an equivalent mistake to underestimate their continuing power to move us—indeed sometimes to move us to tears—as we contemplate their beauty and magnificence.

Some of the crown jewels have been discussed in other contexts in this book—Glacier Bay, for example, and the Grand Canyon. In this chapter, let us offer a few more that experts familiar with what the national parks have to offer insist must be included in any family's program to discover America.

To begin at the beginning means a visit to **Yellowstone National Park**. Let us say you decide to go by air, via Bozeman, Montana, one of Yellowstone's gateway cities. Do not pull down the window shade and watch the movie, for, suddenly, outside your tiny plexiglas porthole in the airliner that has for hours been droning above the patterned fields of the Great Plains, there will appear, just opposite a wingtip, a looming vision: the bright massif of the Absarokas, a towering curtain of folded mountains so magically high they are scarcely to be believed. And beyond them more mountains rise, and mountains beyond mountains, creating a complex of ranges and plateaus dimming into the cerulean distance of the afternoon. So abruptly, so decisively does the place emerge from the American flatlands, so vast and unexpected is it, that it might be a different country, a walled arcanum holding unimaginable secrets.

And that is true; it is, and it does.

At the center of this great hunk of mountain immensity lies the Yellowstone Park, so named after a river rising within it that has carved a great chasm through yellow stone before it tumbles out of the mountains to roll with smooth, deep power into the plains. Feeding the river is the largest high-mountain lake in North America: 20 miles long, 14 miles wide, and 320 feet from top to bottom at the deepest point. These waters, Yellowstone Lake, take up only a corner of the central portion of the park, which is a plateau, a huge, thousand-square-mile caldera—a collapsed volcano—with a crust so thin that the seething core of the earth itself is revealed in spouting geysers, hundreds of pools of boiling water, a thousand vents of sulfurous steam, constituting the greatest collection of geothermal features found anywhere in the world. And all around, the vast forests and limitless meadows hold animals so large their weight may be calculated by the ton; birds so big their wingspread is a matter of yards, not feet or inches; and in the rivers heavy-bodied trout that skim and surge and dance jewel-bright on their tails.

It took 50 years for the wonder of this country to be believed by the outside world, after John Colter and the mountain men told of it. Many do not believe it yet. The only solution is to see for yourself. It was, and is, America's way of saying: Europe, eat your heart out.

What needs to be understood about Yellowstone is that it stands at the center of perhaps the largest relatively intact area of wild nature left in the

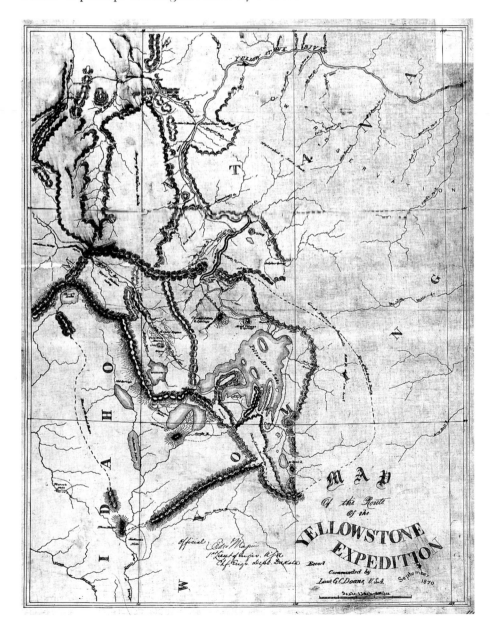

Here, the map used by Lieutenant Gustavus C. Doane during his 1870 expedition to the Yellowstone region. Doane and five soldiers provided a military escort for businessman Nathaniel P. Langford and several other prominent Montana citizens. The party spent a month in the Upper Yellowstone and coined the names of some of the area's natural wonders—Old Faithful, Devil's Den, and Crystal Falls.

temperate zone of the entire world. This is the "Greater Yellowstone Ecosystem," which, at 21,000 square miles, is a third again larger than Switzerland. The ecosystem contains not only Yellowstone National Park but also Grand Teton National Park to the south, plus three wildlife refuges and substantial parts of seven national forests. All of this vast area, with its unique geothermal features, is what sustains the remarkable biological diversity that greets the visitor to Yellowstone.

The incredible ebullitions of Old Faithful—the geyser that goes off every 78 minutes (or so)—are more than just a sideshow in the functioning of the Yellowstone ecosystem. The geothermal features in the park are fun and remarkable and not to be missed for their own sakes, but were it not for them the world's largest species of waterfowl, the trumpeter swan, might now be extinct in the coterminous United States. This 20-pound white giant with a wingspan of eight feet made an easy target for gunners, who could knock it

Carved by ancient volcanic eruptions, the Grand Canyon of the Yellowstone, left, offers a glimpse of Earth's interior, the river's waterfalls highlighting the boundaries of lava flows and thermal zones. Above, sunset on the Firehole River, which runs north through Yellowstone's geyser basins.

Yellowstone features the world's greatest concentrations of geysers, including Castle geyser, above, and some 300 others, about 60 percent of the world's total. Geysers flash water and steam when surface water, having seeped into porous rock layers and become superheated, intermittently shoots to the surface through constricted underground fissures.

down in great numbers as it flew overhead on its annual migration. There was a good living to be made selling swans' down at high prices for the pillows and comforters of the wealthy.

By 1932, the known population of these birds had been reduced to 69 individuals. About 25 of them lived on lakes and ponds in Yellowstone, and the rest at Red Rock Lakes, now a wildlife refuge adjacent to the park. Here the swans were safe because the waters of the lakes, courtesy of the same geothermal phenomena that make Old Faithful do its thing, stayed warm all winter. Thus this relative handful of swans was spared the need to migrate south through a hail of birdshot. These days it is illegal to kill a trumpeter swan, and, thanks to Yellowstone's underground heating system, the number of individuals now stands at about 400 in the Yellowstone ecosystem, a main source for the regeneration of the species. The total population of trumpeters in the United States and Canada is presently believed to be about 10,000.

The creature that perhaps bespeaks this ecosystem more eloquently than any other is the grizzly bear, "the beast that walks on sacred paws," as sea-

Clear water reveals the natural plumbing of Morning Glory pool, left, in Yellowstone's Upper Geyser Basin. The park's abundant geothermal features also warm the waters of the Firehole and Madison rivers, allowing trumpeter swans, above, to remain through the winter.

sonal ranger and bear expert Barbara Pettinga puts it. Humans and grizzly bears get along so badly that a sound assumption can be made that where the bear survives, nature still has the upper hand. And the bear does survive, though it is a close thing, even at Yellowstone. In 1800, wildlife biologists estimate, 100,000 grizzlies roamed the plains and mountains of the West. Today in the coterminous states only a few hundred remain, about half of them living in the greater Yellowstone region.

The thing to know about the grizzly is that he (or more likely she) will at one moment pay no attention to you and at another will charge, which means that something like a third of a ton of fury is coming toward you at 40 miles an hour. Those Yellowstone visitors lucky enough to go on a "bear walk" with Barbara Pettinga will hear of her own close brush with death when a female grizzly knocked her down, biting deeply into the flesh of her

Yellowstone's distinctive and varied natural habitats support a rich array of flora and fauna, including algae, right, in the runoff channels of an Upper Geyser Basin hot spring, and, opposite, clockwise from top, recently reintroduced gray wolves; common black bears, which share this domain with their endangered cousins, the grizzlies; one of the larger wild populations of bison; and moose.

legs and abdomen, and flipped her over three times with its paws. Had Pettinga not pretended to be dead during the assault, the chances are she would not have survived it. The odds that a summer visitor will actually encounter one of these fearsome creatures, however, are about one in twenty. And yet the presence of the bears is everywhere to be seen—in scat, tufts of fur, the clawed bark of a lodgepole pine.

Of the big animals, the easier targets for tourists' telephoto camera lenses will be buffalo and moose, although they, too, will charge. In fact, there are more serious injuries to humans from buffalo than from bears.

For tens of thousands of years, the Yellowstone ecosystem was dominated by three large predators—the grizzly, the mountain lion, and the gray wolf. While not plentiful, the first two of the "big three" have endured. But the wolf, at the instigation of hunters and stockmen, was purposefully exterminated by park authorities by the mid-1930s. Recently a more enlightened understanding of the role of the wolf in the ecosystem has led to an effort to

reintroduce this absent predator. In the wolfless decades since extermination, Yellowstone has become overrun by coyotes, which have filled the wolf's niche, and by elk, which the wolf had kept in check (but coyotes have not), the result being an overgrazed range. At this writing, wildlife biologists have released seven breeding pairs of wolves imported from Canada into remote areas of the park. In time, they hope that these animals might produce a pack of about 50 wolves. Indeed, one female has already given birth to eight pups. There's some hope, too, that the introduction of the wolves will help the grizzly, since a grizzly will chase a wolf off a carcass any chance it gets. Thus, more wolves killing more elk may result in more grizzly food and therefore more grizzlies and a healthier elk herd into the bargain.

Visitors will not see the wolves, which are shy creatures with humans. No human has been seriously attacked by a healthy (that is, non-rabid) wolf. But the nighttime howl will return, the yip-yip-yiparoo that to a wildlife ecologist is as beautiful as a Bach cantata. It is a song that means that Yellowstone is once again complete.

A crown jewel right next to Yellowstone in the tiara of the park system is **Yosemite National Park,** which in the view of many offers the most magnificent mountain-landscape scenery in all of North America. Teddy Roosevelt, accepting no qualifications, called it "the most beautiful place on earth." And certainly its great champion, the Scots-born conservationist John Muir (1838–1914), thought so. He devoted much of his life to its preservation, and founded a citizen organization to help him do it: the Sierra Club, now a half-million members strong.

The centerpiece of Yosemite park, and the object of all the aesthetic attention, is Yosemite Valley. Here was Muir's natural cathedral if ever there was one. He described it as "so compactly and harmoniously arranged that the valley, comprehensively seen, looks like an immense hall or temple lighted from above." With its encircling peaks, the valley is small in area, and yet it gives the impression of immensity. Gouged out by glaciers, Yosemite Valley is surrounded by nearly vertical granitic mountain walls. El Capitan rises 3,593 feet from the valley floor; North Dome, 3,562 feet; Sentinel Rock, 3,068 feet. Yosemite Falls, at 2,435 feet the highest in North America, spills into the valley in three sensational, arcing leaps. And this is only one of the waterfalls in the park, many of which enter the valley at various places. A total of *nine* Yosemite waterfalls, ranging from 300 feet to more than 2,000 feet, are all much higher than Niagara, which is 186 feet.

While it is difficult to leave the valley for other destinations in the park, there is much else to see in what Muir called the "Range of Light" that was "surely the brightest and best of all the Lord has built." A 30-mile drive takes you to Glacier Point, where the valley and the falls and the range behind them are spread out in panorama. At the southern end of the park is the Mariposa Grove with towering redwoods (*Sequoia gigantea*), the largest living things on Earth. The Grizzly Giant, a tree born in 700 B.C., before Romulus founded Rome, is thought to be the oldest individual tree of this species. A visit to Muir's Tuolumne Meadows reveals a series of "flowery

Scenes of yesteryear at Yosemite: above left, Hetch Hetchy Valley before the O'Shaughnessy Dam was completed in 1923; left, Harold Bryant, considered by many the father of the National Park Service's interpretative program, conducting a nature walk in Yosemite Valley in the early 1920s; top, Yosemite waitress Kitty Tatch and friend on an overhang at Glacier Point about 1900; and, above, a Stanley steamer—only the second automobile to enter Yosemite—chugs through the park in 1900.

lawns," as he described them, embowered by forests and encompassed by mountains. At 8,600 feet, these are the largest subalpine meadows in the Sierra Nevadas, and are a jumping-off place for both day hikes and back-packing trips.

Sadly, one of the most spectacular features of the park cannot be seen, at least not as John Muir saw it. It is the Hetch Hetchy Valley, which rivaled the Yosemite Valley in sublimity and yet was more intimate and charming. "One of Nature's rarest and most precious mountain temples," said Muir. Since 1923, when O'Shaughnessy Dam was completed, the valley has been at the bottom of a reservoir constructed to supply the city of San Francisco with water and power. Muir fought tirelessly to save the valley from the boosters and entrepreneurs who stood to gain economically from the project.

> These temple destroyers [raged Muir with Calvinist fury], devotees
> of ravaging commercialism, seem to have a perfect contempt
> for nature, and, instead of lifting their eyes to the God of the
> Mountains, lift them to the almighty dollar. Dam Hetch Hetchy!
> As well dam for water tanks the people's cathedrals and churches;
> for no holier temple has ever been consecrated by the heart of man.

In the end, after a dozen years of unremitting effort, Muir lost the battle of Hetch Hetchy, at the cost, many believe, of his own life. The compensating factor was that his inspired rhetoric, as well as his sacrifice, gave prominence to the movement to preserve the magnificent wild places in America, and led directly to the establishment in 1916 of a National Park "Service" to manage them. Such a bureau could provide for the defense of our national treasures from within the government just as the Sierra Club and other citizen groups could provide for it from without. Said Muir: "The battle for conservation will go on endlessly. It is part of the universal warfare between right and wrong."

Although the West is the site of many of the crown jewels—Sequoia-Kings Canyon, Crater Lake, Mount Rainier, Olympic, Glacier, Big Bend, Zion, Grand Canyon—there are Eastern ones, too. They are fewer in number, however, since by the time the national park idea came into being, Eastern land was settled and parks could not be carved out of the public domain as they were in the West. Most of the Eastern land for parks had to be bought. Luckily, there were philanthropists and enlightened state legislatures to buy it.

The first park thus created was on Mount Desert Island, Maine. **Acadia National Park** was designated a national monument in 1916 as "Sieur de Monts," in recognition of its discovery by Champlain in 1604 and of the French Jesuit mission and colony established there soon after, in 1613. In 1919 Congress voted to make Mount Desert a national park, and named it for

The sunset's rays burnish the top of El Capitan as the Merced River, carrying snowmelt from the High Sierra, follows the path carved by ice-age glaciers as they traveled down the Giant's Stairway to Yosemite Valley.

Theodore Roosevelt called Yosemite "the most beautiful place on earth." Indeed, Mother Nature has created breathtaking scenes here, including Matterhorn Crest, right; Half Dome, below; and Vernal Falls, opposite.

With Half Dome in the distance, boulders known as glacial erratics—so called because they were displaced by the movement of glaciers—resemble so many giant marbles on Yosemite National Park's Olmsted Point.

the Marquis de Lafayette. In 1929 it was renamed Acadia, the French term for what are now the Canadian maritime provinces (and a part of the state of Maine) before the region was taken over by the British in the 1750s and the Acadians deported—some of them to Louisiana, where they are still known as Cajuns.

A century later, steamers from New York and Boston began to put in at Bar Harbor, the largest town on the island, and Mount Desert soon became an artists' colony and a premier retreat for the wealthy. They chose a good place, for nowhere does the sea meet the land on the East Coast of the United States quite so dramatically as it does along the shoreline of Maine. And nowhere in Maine is the meeting quite so impressive as at Mount Desert Island.

The island's name is French, *Mont Desert*, and means "wilderness mountain." Even though the area has been settled for nearly four centuries,

Rising nearly 8,100 feet above sea level in Guadalupe Mountains National Park, Texas, El Capitan, left—not to be confused with the formation of the same name at Yosemite—was covered by a vast tropical ocean 250 million years ago. The Chisos Mountains, below left, reach heights of more than 7,000 feet in Big Bend National Park, Texas, which is located along the U.S.-Mexico border where the Rio Grande River turns sharply to the north. Below, Cattail Falls drains water from the Chisos.

Opposite, dawn breaks over the Teton Range in Grand Teton National Park, Wyoming. Farther west, on Washington's Olympic Peninsula, Olympic National Park features the magnificent Hoh Rain Forest, above left, and 57 miles of Pacific coastline, including Taylor Point, above. At left (center), the world's largest known living thing, the General Sherman tree, in Sequoia National Park's Giant Forest, California.

At right, the intricate shapes of slickrock—wind- or water-smoothed sandstone—in Glen Canyon National Recreation Area, just north of the Utah-Arizona border. Below, other kinds of sandstone form the colorful strata of West Temple, in Zion National Park, Utah. Opposite, the waters of Zion's North Creek scour natural pools.

Waves pound the coast at Otter Point, below, in Acadia National Park, Maine, while the lofty summit of the park's Cadillac Mountain, opposite, overlooks Frenchman Bay.

the sense of wild landscape is retained in the interior of the island as well as along its shores. The rocky summits and sheer cliffs, some dropping a hundred feet to the pounding sea, are a creation of the Ice Age. Glaciers cut deep valleys in a granite ridge, only the top of which is seen today, and scraped the ancient rock clean. Then, when the ice retreated, the sea level rose to drown the shoreline, creating a fjord (Somes Sound) that extends to the center of the island, plus myriad bays, inlets, promontories, and island outliers. Where the glacier-sculpted valleys were closed off by terminal moraines, long, thin freshwater ponds formed that interleave with the granite ridges.

The result of all this geological commotion, together with the plant and animal life that adapted to the rugged coastal environment after the commotion was over, is a stunningly beautiful and biologically rich landscape

Nature's Nation

Ancient glaciers carved the rocky shore of Bass Harbor Head, right, and Schoodic Point, below, in Acadia National Park.

On the southernmost tip of Mount Desert Island, Acadia's Bass Harbor Head lighthouse faces the Atlantic Ocean. It is one of five lighthouses the U.S. Coast Guard maintains in the area to help ships navigate the coast's treacherous rocks and fog. The French explorer Samuel de Champlain, who named the island, ran aground here in 1604.

whose complexity conceals what is, for a national park, a relatively modest size. It bespeaks New England.

It also bespeaks an American trait that is less well-known: land philanthropy. Until the early 1900s, all the land on Mount Desert was privately owned, much of it in the large holdings of wealthy New Englanders who summered there. But, as Henry David Thoreau wrote in his 1852 essay "Walking," "To enjoy a thing exclusively is commonly to exclude yourself from the true enjoyment of it." Heeding this dictum, the truth of which is known to anyone who is blessed with the deed and title to a beautiful landscape, a group of wealthy conservationists met in 1901 to discuss how Mount Desert might be protected in the public's behalf, for even then the island was threatened by tawdry commercial development. The group included Charles W. Eliot, president of Harvard; William Lawrence, bishop of Mass-

Fog rolls through Newfound Gap in Great Smoky Mountains National Park. It is here that the Appalachian Trail intersects Newfound Gap Road, which traverses the park from Cherokee, North Carolina, to Gatlinburg, Tennessee.

achusetts; and George B. Dorr, a wealthy and idealistic Boston Brahmin. The group obtained a charter from the state of Maine to create a public reservation, and sought gifts of land and money to achieve it—most notably from John D. Rockefeller. In 1913 Dorr went to Washington to persuade President Wilson to have the federal government take over the land the philanthropists had assembled. It did, resulting in what is now Acadia National Park, visited by more than 2.5 million people every year.

One of the Rockefeller family legacies, besides the land and money John D. contributed to the park, is a 57-mile network of carriage roads. Built between 1915 and 1933, the narrow roads wind through the bouldery uplands, along the ponds, and down to the sea cliffs. This was no place for automobiles, Rockefeller believed, and he was right. The roads were built with exquisite care of fitted stone. The system, which includes 17 stone bridges and two gatehouses, is designed to provide the best possible panoramas, as well as more intimate natural scenes. The park service now maintains these roads for non-motorized traffic, and has augmented them with 120 miles of trails so that the park visitor's automobile can be parked and the island enjoyed as it should be, afoot or on a bicycle.

Although Acadia National Park, at 40,000 acres, is about one-fiftieth the size of Yellowstone, it is no less a crown jewel. Shortly after its designation, national park champion Robert Sterling Yard said it should be seen as "our standard-bearer for National Park making in the East." A well-known author, editor, and highly visible national park proponent, Yard was, as historian Alfred Runte describes him, a zealot in maintaining the highest possible (read "Western") standards for national park designation. And yet he conceded that the relatively tiny unit on Mount Desert "included National Park essentials in full measure." And that is true; it does.

Straddling the border of North Carolina and Tennessee, along what writer Harry Middleton has called "the spine of time," the Appalachian highlands, is the largest of the Eastern national parks north of the Everglades (which is coming up next). At half a million acres, **Great Smoky Mountains National Park** offers a substantial patch of old-growth Eastern forest as well as some of the highest mountain summits east of the Mississippi.

Like Acadia, the Great Smoky park is made up of land that had to be purchased from private owners. Protecting the Smokies from the ravages of large-scale logging that had begun in the late 19th century was the idea of a St. Louis, Missouri, librarian named Horace Kephardt, who had visited the mountains for his health in 1904. Over the next 20 years he promoted his cause to Congress and the legislatures of Tennessee and North Carolina. At length, in 1926, Congress enacted legislation authorizing Great Smoky Mountains National Park (as well as Shenandoah National Park, in Virginia), but appropriated no money for land purchase. In 1927 both North Carolina and Tennessee voted the funds, and began purchasing land for a park. Once again the Rockefeller family came through with a substantial gift of money. Lumber companies were bought out, along with small farms, and

A hardwood forest along the Little Pigeon River in Great Smoky Mountains National Park. Heavily forested, the park is now an International Biosphere Reserve area.

the park was officially established in 1934 when the states transferred the land they had assembled to the National Park Service.

The park's designation was based on its conformance with the standards set for many Western parks—mountain topography. Accordingly, most visitors will take the scenic drive over the crest of the Smokies or head for Clingman's dome (6,542 feet elevation). But it is the Appalachian *forest* that makes the park so distinctive. There are several forest types here. At the highest elevations stands the spruce-fir forest, an Ice Age remnant that more properly belongs in New England and Canada. Also at the higher elevations is the northern hardwood forest of beech and birch. Elsewhere, beautiful evergreen hemlock forests grow along streams, and pine and oak forests can be found on drier slopes.

Examples of the most remarkable forest community of all, the old-growth mixed mesophytic woodlands, can be found in some of the mid-elevation coves in the park, especially on the western (Tennessee) slope. The term "mixed mesophytic" was coined in 1916 by the pioneering botanist E. Lucy Braun, who studied these Southern deciduous woodlands all her life.

(*Meso* is the combining form of "mesic," the word botanists use to describe a growing environment that is middling—not too hot or cold, wet or dry. *Phytic* means, simply, plant. And *mixed* means that there are many dominants rather than a few.) While most forests are of two or three dominant types of trees, the mixed mesophytic can have a dozen or more species making up a canopy a hundred to a hundred and fifty feet high—tulip poplar, buckeye, sweetgum, and several kinds of magnolias, oaks, basswoods, hickories, and maples.

Given the large number of canopy and sub-canopy species in the mixed mesophytic—80 in all—this is a kind of temperate-zone tropical rain forest. The coves, untouched by the glaciers and at a high enough elevation in these old mountains to have escaped inundation by ancient seas, contain the oldest woodlands on Earth, with predecessor trees dating to 100 million years ago when the angiosperms—flowering, broad-leaved trees—first evolved. Lucy Braun described the mixed mesophytic as "the most complex and the oldest association" of all deciduous forests. "From it, and from its ancestral progenitor, the mixed Tertiary forest as a whole, all other climaxes of the de-

Autumn foliage along the Blue Ridge Parkway near Bull Gap, North Carolina. This scenic, 469-mile parkway follows the crest of the Blue Ridge Mountains at an average height of about 3,000 feet above sea level.

Right, autumn leaves glow over moss- and lichen-covered boulders at Craggy Gardens along the Blue Ridge Parkway in North Carolina. Opposite, a dreamlike view of the Appalachian Trail at Brown's Gap, Shenandoah National Park, Virginia. This scenic trail winds some 2,000 miles through the Appalachian Mountains from Mount Katahdin, in central Maine, to Springer Mountain, in northern Georgia.

ciduous forest have arisen," Braun wrote. In effect, then, these protected coves produced the "mother forest" that re-created all of the Eastern woodlands after the vast climate changes over long periods of geological time wiped out existing forests elsewhere.

If the initial impulse to create Great Smoky Mountains National Park was much the same as that which led to the creation of the big Western parks, a more sophisticated view of what was important to preserve was growing in the national park movement as the 20th century unfolded: an appreciation for the variety and intricacies of nature rather than its impressive, picturesque geomorphologies. This appreciation reached its zenith in the Eastern United States, not the West—in the creation of **Everglades National Park,** where the topography is absolutely flat (highest elevation: eight feet), but where nature, in this semitropical place, demonstrates a delicate, sometimes hidden, complexity. The shift in emphasis was clearly expressed in

President Harry S Truman's address at the dedication of the park in 1947. "Here are no lofty peaks seeking the sky," he said, "no mighty glaciers or rushing streams wearing away the uplifted land. Here is land, tranquil in its quiet beauty, serving not as the source of water but as the last receiver of it. To its natural abundances we owe the spectacular plant and animal life that distinguishes this place from all others in our country."

The abundant water of which Truman spoke comes from the torrential rains that fall on south Florida. Much of it collects in Lake Okeechobee, at 700 square miles our largest freshwater body aside from the Great Lakes, and moves southward through what Marjorie Stoneman Douglas, a key figure in Everglades conservation, called "the river of grass." It is a hundred miles of saw grass that the water flows through, the largest saw-grass marsh in the world, totaling some ten million acres, of which about one-seventh— 1.5 million acres—falls within the boundaries of Everglades National Park.

It is the grass river, scores of miles wide but only two feet deep, that the American alligator finds so agreeable. No place else can this impressive creature be found so readily and in such numbers as in the protected Ever-

A dwarf-cypress pond in Everglades National Park, Florida. Located within the world's largest saw-grass marsh, the park stretches for 1.5 million acres across the flattest of terrains, its highest elevation only eight feet above sea level.

glades of the park. Here the largest known alligator is said to have measured 19 feet in length. Those found today in the park top out at 12 or 13 feet.

When the river begins to dry up, as it does to a greater or lesser extent every year, the alligators dig "gator holes" for themselves, and in the process create miniature ecosystems that are crucial to maintaining the dynamic natural balances of the Everglades in its entirety. The alligator, deploying its powerful tail and snout, hollows out what becomes a small pond for itself, but it is quickly joined by fish, turtles, snails, and other creatures also wishing to find safety from the drying sun. In this way, the alligator acts as the "keeper of the Everglades," for the living things its excavation has protected can once again go forth (if they have not been eaten) to repopulate the larger Everglades ecosystem when the rains return.

Another Everglades Park ecosystem-within-an-ecosystem may be found in the hardwood hammocks, which rise like small islands from the saw-grass sea. The word "hammock" is from the Indian *hammocka*, meaning "garden place," and that is an apt description. The hammocks, which have an elevation only a few feet above the level of the grass, provide dry footing for a whole different set of plants and animals. Past the periphery of thick bushes that encircle the hammock, the interior becomes a somewhat open woodland, with sunlight filtering through the canopy of slash pine, royal palms, live oaks, and a tree called the *gumbo limbo*. The region's rich variety of waterfowl feed at the edges, and within the cool interior the few mammals the Everglades supports can find a home—white-tailed deer, raccoons, possibly even the rare Florida panther.

For human visitors, perhaps the most remarkable denizen of the hammocks is a tiny tree-snail. But these are snails with a difference, for they seem like jewelry fastened to the trunks of the lysiloma trees. The snails—*Liguus fasciatus*—come in as many as 50 distinct patterns, with colors ranging from vivid topaz to deep ruby arrayed in dazzlingly varied spiral bands.

Toward the places where the fresh water mingles with the salt, pine forests grow along a coastal ridge. Inland and adjacent to the park lies the Big Cypress Swamp, which itself contributes to the intricately layered association of plants and animals in south Florida. In the National Audubon Society's Corkscrew Swamp Sanctuary is the largest remaining stand of bald cypress, supporting a large, though dwindling, woodstork rookery. The stork is seen as an indicator species of the environmental health of the Everglades region, for its breeding regimen is easily disrupted by human activities, such as the building of residential subdivisions spreading out from coastal cities and wetland drainage for agriculture in the northern part of the glades.

Finally, at the outflow of the grass river are the magnificent and utterly essential mangrove swamps. In the Everglades, three species of mangrove grow, the most spectacular being the red mangrove, whose roots descend from several feet up on the tree down to the water like a tangle of branches. The tangle provides feeding and breeding places for myriad species of fish and amphibians upon which waterfowl feed.

This meager description by no means encompasses nature's richness in Everglades National Park. It has only barely hinted at the highlights. A visitor could, for example, become fascinated by the manatees, the mammalian

The American alligator (*Alligator mississippiensis*) is found throughout the Everglades, thriving in this great "river of grass," as Everglades conservationist Marjorie Stoneman Douglas termed the saw-grass marsh in the 1940s.

The Everglades' ecosystem supports such endangered species as the manatee, top, the bald eagle, and the Florida panther. Opposite, a cypress stand in Big Cypress National Preserve, which borders Everglades National Park.

"sea cows" that the sailors of old took for mermaids. These mermaids, ugly as sin and yet charming in their way, are found at the park. So, too, are the anhingas, the "snake birds" that swim with their bodies below the surface of the water; the brilliant gallinule; and the endangered snail kite, which feeds only on a certain kind of snail, *Pomacea*, which is easily killed by agricultural chemicals.

With so many species nearing or on the brink of extinction—snail kite, woodstork, Florida panther, American crocodile, loggerhead turtle, bald eagle, manatee, peregrine falcon, indigo snake—the story of the Everglades is the story of last-ditch conservation. While this topic has not heretofore been a motif in this book, it is hard to avoid when talking about such a fragile ecosystem. For nearly a century, conservationists have been striving to save the Everglades, sometimes at the cost of their very lives. Here is where the Audubon Society gained its initial reputation, when the Audubon game wardens cut a romantic swath across the history of wildlife conservation in the early part of this century. The best of the warden stories, as recounted by Frank Graham, Jr., in his history of the Audubon Society (*Audubon Ark*), is that of Guy Bradley, who, threatened with death at the hands of lawless plume hunters in the wilds of what is now Everglades National Park, confronted a boatful of the evildoers on a July morning in 1905. The hunters invited Bradley aboard, and then murdered him. Florida justice, being notoriously weak, failed to convict the murderers, adding a special luster to Bradley's martyrdom. "He gave his life for the cause to which he was pledged," reads his weathered tombstone on the windy ridge of Cape Sable, at the southernmost part of the park. President Theodore Roosevelt sent a letter of condolence to the newly formed organization—now the National Audubon Society—that had employed brave warden Bradley.

Today, with threats to the park even greater than those posed by the plume hunters of yesteryear, what is required is less physical courage than political courage, for headlong economic development of south Florida will, unless it is significantly modified, deal a mortal blow to plant and animal communities within the park. At times, the ecosystems of the park are starved for water that has been diverted for irrigators, factories, and subdivisions. Alternately, stored up water, laced with agricultural chemicals, is often released at the wrong moment, inundating nesting and feeding sites. High levels of deadly mercury have been found in fish, birds, and alligators throughout the park.

Every park is, to one degree or another, threatened by the incursions of urban development, pollution, and resource exploitation. But this message is especially urgent for the Everglades National Park. How, or whether, the message is received by those who are in control of national park policy and by the powers that be in south Florida will determine the future of the fantastic web of life that the Everglades reveals. And if the Everglades cannot be saved, then we must wonder about the integrity of the rest of the system of national parks—both the crown jewels and lesser gems—that has so lovingly been created over the last century and a quarter and that so perfectly expresses what is fine and good and *different* about the American relationship to wild nature.

TOWARD A MORE PERFECT UNION

The mystic chords of memory, stretching from
every battlefield and patriot grave to every living
heart and hearthstone all over this broad land,
will yet swell the chorus of the Union when
again touched, as surely they will be, by the
better angels of our nature.

—Abraham Lincoln
First Inaugural Address

Just as our national parks serve to measure our relations to the glories of
nature, so, too, do they record our relations to one another, by com-
memorating in landscapes and buildings the milestones that have figured
prominently in the life of the United States of America. More than a hundred parks, monuments, and historic sites mark the progress of this continental nation where the world's most significant experiment in representa-
tive government and democratic politics—not invariably admirable, but
always instructive—has been underway now for more than two centuries.

It began on July 2, 1776 (yes, July 2), when the Second Continental
Congress, meeting in Philadelphia, approved a motion put forward by
Richard Henry Lee of Virginia nearly a month before. The motion declared
that "these United Colonies are, and of right ought to be, free and indepen-
dent States." There and then the cord binding the colonies to Britain was
cut, and new bands (Jefferson's word), however inchoate, were created—

Cemetery Hill, Gettysburg National
Military Park, Pennsylvania. Here, in July
1863, General George C. Meade's federal
troops repelled the northernmost
offensive of General Robert E. Lee's
Army of Northern Virginia.

Built between 1732 and 1756, Philadelphia's State House, known today as Independence Hall, is revered as the place where the Declaration of Independence was adopted in 1776, the Articles of Confederation were ratified in 1781, and the U.S. Constitution was drafted in 1787.

bands that would unite the colonies with one another and in time create a Union, with a capital U.

The motion came about because for a decade previous the colonists had been sorely tried—often stupidly so on the part of the British king and parliament. After the British had won the French and Indian War (1754–63), in which Americans had fought bravely, the mother country, beset by debts from the war, for the first time imposed direct taxes on the colonies, whereas before revenue had been derived only from import duties. The most notorious of the new taxes was the infamous Stamp Act of 1765, which required that any kind of public document or paper—broadsides, legal documents, commercial bills, playing cards, university diplomas—bear a stamp. And this new tax was no minor assessment: the tax had to be paid in sterling, not Colonial currency, which effectively tripled the impact. Even so, many Americans were inclined to accept the new taxes as their fair share of the war debts, for the victory benefited them by securing their northern and western frontiers. But Parliament had made the fatal tactical error of including newspapers in the Stamp Act, and requiring publishers to pay fourpence sterling not per issue, but for every sheet of every issue. The publishers, in turn, vehemently condemned the tax on their front pages, effectively stirring up such resentment about the whole idea of direct taxation that, in the end, there was no turning back. Indeed, if Parliament had simply left newspapers out of the act, the whole of American history might have been different.

Immediately, the growing American merchant class, led by the unremittingly radical Bostonian Samuel Adams and his associates, exploited the growing resentment over taxation by boycotting British goods and organizing the "Sons of Liberty" in the port cities. Posing as toughs and hoodlums, the "Liberty Boys" broke into the Stamp Tax offices, destroyed the hated stamps, and terrorized the collection agents into resigning. In October 1765 a "Stamp Act Congress" was convened in which nine colonies, meeting in New York, agreed that the British law had illegally imposed taxation over the heads of the colonial legislatures and that the tax was improper also because those who were taxed had no representation on the taxing body, the British Parliament. They sent King George a firm message to this effect and declared that the Stamp Act should be repealed forthwith. The protest was an important, far-reaching action, with political implications that were much greater than the immediate economic concerns occasioned by taxation. For this group of men constituted our very first homegrown *congress*, whose success at reaching consensus demonstrated that the far-flung colonies of America could actually work together in their own behalf.

Parliament repealed the Stamp Tax the following year, with the blessing of George III. The Americans had won their point. But in 1767 England imposed new import duties under the Townshend Acts, which called for their strict enforcement. The Townshend Acts obviated the "taxation without representation" issue, but failed to address what was really going on in America. The colonies were beginning to think of themselves as belonging to one another, rather than to Great Britain. In Boston, Sam Adams escalated the pressure against the British. Protests mounted, boycotts of British goods were reinstated, and the number of incidents between the Liberty Boys and British troops increased. In 1768 the British retaliated by dissolving the Massachusetts Assembly, and on March 5, 1770, the "Boston Massacre," in which exasperated Redcoats fired into a crowd of protesters, claimed the lives of five men. It wasn't much of a massacre, certainly not by French and Indian War standards, but it was enough to make everyone's blood boil throughout the colonies.

Back in England, Parliament realized that the Townshend Acts were causing more trouble than they were bringing in revenue, and thus repealed them—coincidently on the same day as the Boston Massacre. There was but one exception to the repeal—tea—producing yet another opportunity for Sam Adams, the Sons of Liberty, and other rebellious types to turn up the heat another notch. In 1774 British tea ships were turned away from most American ports in protest, but cleverly allowed into Boston Harbor, whereupon a mob disguised as Indians and Negro slaves boarded them and consigned 342 huge chests of tea to the bottom of the bay. And that—the "Boston Tea Party"—changed everything. Whereas British policy had been merely stupid before, it now became vindictive. "The die is now cast," King George wrote to his Prime Minister, Lord North. "The Colonies must either submit or triumph."

Lord North was all too willing to put the colonies to the test via a series of punitive laws, enacted by Parliament in 1774, that Americans called the "Intolerable Acts." They included the Boston Port Act, which blockaded Boston Harbor until the colony chose to reimburse the British for the dumped tea, and the "Quartering Act," which provided that royal governors could commandeer private residences for billeting soldiers without a by-your-leave. Such petulance did not exactly calm revolutionary fervor, but instead led to the calling (on September 5, 1774) of the First Continental Congress, held at Carpenter's Hall in Philadelphia. Six weeks later, the 55 delegates from 12 colonies (Georgia was not present) voted to create a "Continental Association" that would bar the importation and use of British goods and that set forth a petition of grievances to be sent to King George. Their next meeting was scheduled for May 10, 1775, to consider what to do if the grievances were not satisfied. Significantly, the colonists were not, by any means, declaring independence at this point. They wished only for the British government to recognize their rights.

Meanwhile, the Massachusetts colony, having had its assembly dissolved, was, under Sam Adams's prodding, becoming more defiant. In an effort to forestall open rebellion, British General George Gage sent a column of troops out to rural Concord, where the colonials had stored munitions. Forewarned by Paul Revere and others that the British were on their way, a ragtag group of colonial militia calling themselves the Minutemen intercepted the Redcoats on the common of the town of Lexington, adjacent to Concord. (Both are now suburbs of Boston.) "Disperse, ye rebels, disperse!" cried the correct General Gage. Then someone—and no one has ever known who it might have been—fired a shot at the Redcoats from behind a stone wall. It was the shot, declaimed Ralph Waldo Emerson many years later in a famous poem, that was "heard round the world."

Locally, the shot precipitated a brief skirmish that left five Minutemen dead, after which the Redcoats continued on to Concord, where they destroyed some supplies, encountering yet another group of Minutemen. Then the British withdrew to Boston, having lost 200 men to the American stonewall snipers whose guerrilla tactics gave the Minutemen the advantage over the better-armed Redcoats. The date was April 19, 1775. The Revolutionary War had begun.

In Boston, the events leading up to the war are commemorated at **Boston National Historical Park,** including the Old North Church ("One if by land...") and Paul Revere's house as well as many public buildings associated with the Revolution. In Concord, the **Minute Man National Historical Park** preserves and interprets the first engagement of the war, including what happened along four miles of the "Battle Road" between Lexington and Concord.

For the British, the timing of this first battle was inopportune. The Second Continental Congress was to meet less than a month later. Given the recent events, the delegates wasted no time in appointing George Washington commander in chief, instructing him to raise a Continental Army forthwith.

Throughout 1775, even while the fighting was escalating, the Americans made a final effort at reconciliation, but it was spurned by the British. At last the delegates in Philadelphia came to see that declaring independence was the only course open to them. "Every quiet method for peace hath been ineffectual," wrote Thomas Paine in *Common Sense*, "and have tended to convince us that nothing flatters vanity or confirms obstinacy in kings more than repeated petitioning." Paine's pamphlet, which sold 150,000 copies, was persuasive. Independence was declared in the motion by Richard Henry Lee.

Then, two days after Lee's procedural motion was accepted, a brilliant 33-year-old Virginia lawyer completed the final draft of the formal declaration he had been working on for a month. After much wrangling it was adopted on July 4 and read from the balcony of Independence Hall to a gathering of citizens on July 8. "We hold these truths to be self-evident," came the words, "that all men are created equal, that they are endowed by their Creator with certain unalienable Rights, that among these are Life, Liberty, and the pursuit of Happiness.—That to secure these rights, Governments are instituted among Men, deriving their just powers from the consent of the governed."

And so, with Thomas Jefferson's ringing sentences, did our great experiment begin.

The Declaration of Independence was the first of our two greatest public documents. The second, also created at Philadelphia, would take another 11 years to bring into being—the Constitution of the United States of America—for independence was one thing, but a functioning government was quite another. First of all, a war had to be fought, and it raged on, up and down the colonies, until 1783. During this time of upheaval a prelusive constitution was created and finally ratified by all the former colonies in 1781—the Articles of Confederation. From the vantage point of historical hindsight, this first constitution was perhaps a necessary step, but it was clearly ineffectual in governing a geographically diffuse set of former colonies. The Articles, in effect, divided the powers of the new nation rather than consolidating them. The central government was weak, operating only on sufferance of the states. But many who stood to prosper from a condition of national disunity refused to accept the obvious defects of the Articles.

Then came Shay's Rebellion. No event was more convincing to a majority of America's new political leadership of the need for an effective central government than this uprising (in the fall and winter of 1786–87) of Massachusetts farmers impoverished by economic depression after the conclusion of the war. The rebels, who wanted the state to print paper money to relieve their debt, were very near to toppling the government in Boston when Massachusetts begged the Confederation for aid. But none was forthcoming. The Congress had neither the money nor the authority to provide it. In the end, law and order prevailed, but the lesson was a powerful one for all the states, revealing the shortcomings of the Articles of Confederation.

Even before Shay's Rebellion matters were getting out of hand. The states were taxing one another's products, prohibiting access to fisheries, and generally acting irresponsibly. At length, the Virginia assembly suggested that the states send delegates to a convention in Annapolis, Maryland, to take up matters of trade regulation. Only five delegations showed up, but among the conferees were two young men who suddenly found themselves in a position of leadership: James Madison of Virginia and Alexander Hamilton of New York. These men were to write, with John Jay, *The Federalist Papers*, a classic disquisition on the way in which a centralized republican government can not only produce a powerful sovereign state but also safeguard its citizens from tyrannical rule.

At Annapolis, Madison and Hamilton understood that the problem was not just trade regulation. What was needed was (in the words of Hamilton's

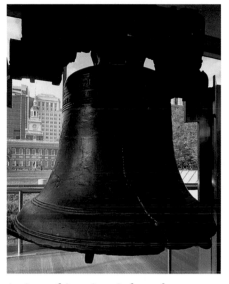

An icon of American independence, the Liberty Bell was commissioned in 1751 by the Pennsylvania Provincial Assembly to hang in the State House, now Independence Hall. Today it hangs in Liberty Bell Pavilion, Independence National Historical Park, Philadelphia.

At the end of a cobblestone street near Independence Hall, Carpenters' Hall was the meeting place of the First Continental Congress in 1774. It is still owned and operated by the Carpenters' Company of Philadelphia.

report) "to render the constitution of the federal government adequate to the exigencies of the Union." The Congress carefully considered this suggestion coming out of Annapolis, and in February 1787 invited the states to send special delegates to Philadelphia to revise the Articles of Confederation in behalf of "the preservation of the Union."

There are some who believe, and with justification, that the product of the ensuing convention was America's greatest achievement. The convention did much more than simply revise the Articles of Confederation to solve commercial problems between the states. As we now know, between May 25 and September 17 of 1787, the men who gathered at Philadelphia somehow managed to hammer out a constitution that would work not only for four million people living in 13 former colonies situated along the Atlantic shore but (as historian Samuel Eliot Morison points out) for 50 states flung across the entire continent, and even half the Pacific Ocean, with a present-day population in the hundreds of millions.

What a distinguished group these delegates were! Most were young (excepting Benjamin Franklin, of course, who was 81), highly educated in the classics as well as the liberal arts, commonsensical, and utterly patriotic in a way that has scarcely been seen since. The Constitution was, says Morison, "a work of genius," and "undoubtedly the most original contribution of the United States to the history and technique of human liberty."

The authors were, to use a term now much in disfavor, America's intellectual elite. We should be grateful that no populist, anti-intellectual opprobrium then attached to the kinds of men chosen for the great task. The opening sentence of their document rings hard and true and without ambiguity: "We the people of the United States," it proclaims, "in order to form a more perfect Union, establish justice, insure domestic tranquility, provide for the common defense, promote the general welfare, and secure the blessings of liberty to ourselves and our posterity, do ordain and establish this Constitution for the United States of America."

The Constitution, being a document of principle rather than mere rules, is admirably brief, briefer in fact than this chapter of the book you are now reading. The last of its seven articles provided that "the ratification of the conventions of nine States shall be sufficient for the establishment of this Constitution between the States so ratifying the same." But ratification was no simple matter, for the Anti-Federalists did not give up easily. Indeed, the 85 *Federalist Papers* were published in New York to convince a single state to approve the new Constitution. Nevertheless, by June 21, 1788, the requisite nine states had ratified, and the Constitution went into effect the following year.

Today, more than two centuries later, at **Independence National Historical Park**, one can stand where these great intellectual achievements of our nation took place. And it is impossible not to be moved. The visitor will hear the echoes of hope and despair in Carpenters' Hall, where the first Continental Congress met in 1774; sense the powerful intellect at work in Declaration House, the reconstructed residence of Jacob Graff, where Jefferson penned his drafts of the Declaration of Independence in 1776; feel jubilation at Independence Square, where the Declaration was first read, and

Toward a More Perfect Union

sense the determination of those men of genius in Independence Hall as they debated, issue by issue, the provisions of their new Constitution. And at the Liberty Bell Pavilion, one can touch this symbol of freedom that rang out in triumph and trepidation in July 1776. Cracked twice, in 1835 and 1846, and threatened in less physical, but metaphorically more consequential, ways by dire constitutional challenges to the Union, the bell with its biblical inscription still has the power to inspire. It reads: "Proclaim Liberty throughout all the Land unto all the Inhabitants Thereof."

The first major challenge to the Union was met, not handily but at least not unvictoriously, by the new nation in the War of 1812–15 with Britain. The causes were complex, relating at the outset to national alignments in Europe that affected and were affected by American shipping interests. The fighting started through a series of ineptitudes on the part of President James Madison (a better Constitution-framer than politician), a bit of trickery on the part of Napoleon, a missed opportunity to avoid armed conflict through diplomacy, and the growth of nationalism fomented by "war hawk" political extremists—mainly southern Republicans (later to be called Democrats).

For many, the war is most notorious because of the gratuitous raid by the British on Washington, the new seat of government. Only a few militia turned out to defend the city, so the British torched all the public buildings, including the White House (then called "The Palace"), though not before the Redcoats helped themselves to a dinner that President and Mrs. Madison were meant to consume. The next target for the raiders was Baltimore, which was better prepared to wage a fight. In that city, at Fort McHenry, despite a nighttime British Naval bombardment, the fort held. By dawn's early light our flag was still there, the star-spangled banner gallantly streaming. The result was a non-victory for the British and a stirring national anthem for the United States of America, the words courtesy of Francis Scott Key, a Washington lawyer who witnessed the event, and the music courtesy of an English drinking song, "To Anacreon in Heaven." The fort is now a unit of the national park system, the **Fort McHenry National Monument and Historic Shrine.**

Much worse was to come. Thomas Jefferson wrote in *Notes on Virginia,* his only book (first published in 1784), of the perils to the republic that the institution of slavery was likely to bring. "I tremble for my country when I reflect that God is just: that his justice cannot sleep forever."

Slavery was already an issue of controversy when Jefferson wrote the Declaration of Independence. When he asserted that "all men are created equal," did he and his colleagues include slaves in the definition of "men"? They did not. In fact, the framers avoided the question as having the potential to spoil the whole federal effort then and there. Jefferson's own ambivalence, even hypocrisy—he opposed slavery but owned 200 slaves—was perhaps indicative of the attitude held by many of our young founding fathers.

As it turned out, though he held national office for nearly 20 years, Jefferson never did have to face his apprehensions about the retribution of a just God for the practice of slavery. In 1790, after returning from France, where he was ambassador, Jefferson was appointed Secretary of State by President Washington and was asked to come to New York, then the capital. He served in that post for three years until unreconcilable differences with Alexander Hamilton arose. Jefferson feared that Hamilton might, if he had his way, so over-centralize the government that it could revert to a monarchy. In 1793 he returned to his beloved estate, Monticello, in Albemarle County, Virginia. He owned, at Monticello and in Bedford County to the southeast, about 10 thousand acres. At 50, Jefferson thought he could devote the rest of his days to what he believed was man's noblest pursuit, farming. As it happened, however, he was required to return to public life in 1796, as Vice President to John Adams. And then he was himself elected President for two terms and was the first President to occupy the White House in the new capital city of Washington.

Jefferson was a polymath—architect, agriculturist, scientist, educator, industrial designer, lawyer, philosopher—and clearly the most impressive political figure in early U.S. history. His achievements were manifold, but perhaps the most profound, considering its influence on the future of the United States, was the transforming of a tiny conglomeration of 13 former colonies whose population clung to the Atlantic shore and looked to Europe as a point of reference to a continental nation that could turn its face decisively the other way: westward. The Ordinance of 1787, enacted by the Congress of the Confederation in Jefferson's absence—the "Northwest Ordinance" that created the Northwest Territories—was based on Jefferson's own draft Ordinance of 1784. And, as President, Jefferson himself presided over the Louisiana Purchase in 1803, which secured for $15 million the middle third of the country—the vast Mississippi-Missouri drainage.

These were massively significant governmental actions, but perhaps the most extraordinary legacy resulted from a single expedition that Jefferson got Congress to approve. The President appointed his private secretary, Captain Meriwether Lewis, age 28, to head it; Lewis, in turn, asked a good friend, a former army officer named William Clark, 33, to become co-leader. The object of the expedition, which Jefferson had first proposed to the Philadelphia Philosophical Society in 1792, was made urgent in the event of the Louisiana Purchase. It was to find a land route to the Pacific, assert territorial claims to the Oregon country, and gather information about the Indians and the natural resources and topography of the far West.

The company set out from St. Louis in May 1804. Two years and three months later, in September 1806, they returned, with the greatest adventure story in American history, all of it faithfully recorded in the incomparable three-volume *History of the Lewis and Clark Expedition*, drawn from the voluminous manuscript journals and field notes gathered by the explorers. The pages are filled with accounts of encounters with thundering buffalo and giant grizzlies, of prairie dogs and wolves, of roaring cataracts and stratospheric mountains; and of people, too: of the death of Sergeant Floyd, after whom they named a river; of Mandan villages and of Sacajawea, the Shoshone

In May 1804 Meriwether Lewis, top, and William Clark, above, set out from St. Louis, Missouri, on their now legendary expedition to the Pacific. In 1978 the National Park Service established the 3,700-mile Lewis and Clark National Historic Trail to commemorate the journey.

In this 1833 sketch, above, Swiss artist Karl Bodmer depicted a Plains scene with the Rocky Mountains in the distance. Traveling some 2,000 miles up the Missouri River with the 1833–34 Western expedition of Prince Maximilian of Wied-Neuwied, Bodmer was one of the first skilled artists to record the natural wonders described by Lewis and Clark.

woman who helped the explorers negotiate the trackless high Rockies. Here is an excerpt, dated April 29, 1805. At this point the party has reached the vicinity where the Yellowstone River enters the Missouri:

We proceeded early, with a moderate wind. Captain Lewis, who was on shore with one hunter, met about eight o'clock two white bears. [These were grizzlies, which sometimes appear blond, in contrast to the eastern black bear, with which the explorers were more familiar.] Of the strength and ferocity of this animal the Indians had given us dreadful accounts. They never attack him but in parties of six or eight persons, and even then are often defeated with a loss of one or more of their party....We are surrounded with deer, elk, buffalo, antelopes, and their companions the wolves, which have become more numerous and make great ravages among them. The hills are here much more rough and high, and almost overhang the banks of the river.

The **Lewis and Clark National Historic Trail**, a part of the national park system (as are 16 other historic and scenic trails), was established in 1978 to mark this journey to the Pacific and back again—including several side trips. For 3,700 miles, highways and roads that run close to the original route through prairies and mountains and along waterways have been mapped

and designated. Along the way, there are roadside markers and museum exhibits telling the story.

The **Jefferson National Expansion Memorial** in St. Louis also celebrates this great adventure, and celebrates, too, the westering vision of our third President. The now-familiar Memorial Arch rises on the Mississippi waterfront, reminding us that St. Louis was the "gateway" to the West. Completed in 1968, the arch is a wonderful tourist attraction. Designed by architect Eero Saarinen, it stands 630 feet tall and is 630 feet wide at the base. Visitors can ride to the top huddled in tiny "tram" capsules for a panoramic view of the city and the two great rivers upon which it was built, the Mississippi and the Missouri.

Centered beneath the legs of the arch is an underground museum, the Museum of Westward Expansion, where one can wander among the exhibits while waiting to ride in the tram, which is often crowded. The museum, in a series of photographic tableaus (by the photographer for this book), tells the story of the Lewis and Clark expedition and of other aspects of westward expansion.

It is not insignificant that only two blocks from the Jefferson National Expansion Memorial is the Old Courthouse—originally the St. Louis County

During the 1833–34 Maximilian expedition, Bodmer made this sketch of buffalo and elk on the Missouri River. It recalls one of Meriwether Lewis's journal entries from 1805: "We saw a vast number of buffalo feeding in every direction around us in the plains, others coming down in large herds to the water at the river."

courthouse, built in 1828. Administratively, the Old Courthouse is a part of the memorial. Here, in 1847 and again in 1850, trials were held to determine the fate of a Negro slave named Dred Scott. The outcome of those trials, most particularly the Supreme Court decision that arose from them, gave substance at last to Jefferson's slavery-fears that "justice cannot sleep forever."

The Dred Scott affair was not the only spark that ignited the obscenely brutal hell-on-earth called the American Civil War. In 1859 the half-mad abolitionist John Brown captured the U.S. arsenal at Harper's Ferry (an event memorialized at **Harper's Ferry National Historical Park**, in West Virginia). Later, when Harriet Beecher Stowe, the author of *Uncle Tom's Cabin*, was introduced to Abraham Lincoln, the grieving, plain-spoken President said: "So you're the little woman who wrote the book that started this great war." But the Dred Scott case made the war impossible to avoid, thanks in substantial part to a decision written by Chief Justice Roger Brooke Taney. The Supreme Court, which heard the case in 1857, affirmed (seven to two) the fugitive slave laws (which by then *required* all U.S. citizens to help authorities capture runaways) and declared that the federal government had no authority to prohibit slavery in new territories, as the Missouri Compromise of 1820 had provided as a means to maintain parity between slave states and free when territories entered the Union.

Dred Scott had been bought (how odd the word seems now!) from the Peter Blow family by a Dr. and Mrs. John Emerson of St. Louis. Scott accompanied Dr. Emerson, a military surgeon, to various "free" states where slavery had been prohibited under the Missouri Compromise. Upon returning to St. Louis in 1842, Scott and his wife, whom he had married in Minnesota, continued to work for the Emersons. But the following year Dr. Emerson died, and his wife, to raise money, "hired out" Dred Scott to other families. This practice, which made Scott's status as mere property so unambiguous, may have been what led him to file suit against Mrs. Emerson in 1846 for his freedom. The basis of the suit was a Missouri doctrine of "once free, always free," which Scott asserted pertained to his case because of his nine-year sojourn with Dr. Emerson. Scott's original owners, the Blow family, provided financial support to their former slave, and the court ruled in 1850 that Scott was a free man.

The freedom was short-lived, however. In 1852 the county court decision was reversed on appeal. Two years later Scott filed suit in the St. Louis Federal Court, which also decided against him, as did the Supreme Court, as we have seen. The chilling language of Chief Justice Taney's decision shows clearly that the great flaw in the Constitution, in which neither the word "Negro" nor "slavery" appears, could no longer be avoided: "[I]f the Constitution recognizes the right of property of the master in a slave, and makes no distinction between that description of property and other property owned by a citizen, no tribunal, acting under the authority of the United States, whether it be legislative, executive or judicial, has a right to draw such a dis-

Firmly planted on the banks of the Mississippi, the 630-foot-tall Gateway Arch salutes St. Louis, the city that once served as the gateway to the West. The arch is part of the National Park Service's Jefferson National Expansion Memorial.

tinction, or deny it the benefit of the provisions and guarantees which have been provided for the protection of private property against the encroachments of the Government."

Given this decision, it became clear that the Union was not becoming "more perfect," as the words of the Preamble to the Constitution had it, but less so. In fact, by 1861, after Lincoln was elected President with the support of the new antislavery Republican Party (the early Republicans were now called Democrats), 11 southern states asserted that as far as they were concerned there was no Union at all. On April 12, 1861, Confederate forces fired on the 85-man federal garrison at Fort Sumter, South Carolina, located in Charleston Harbor. After 34 hours a truce was called, and the federal troops boarded a ship bound for New York. Miraculously, no one was killed on either side, but the war had begun that was to claim more American lives than any other. Today, visitors can reach **Fort Sumter National Monument** via a tour boat leaving from the City Marina in Charleston.

What was the cost of union? In 1854 Lincoln, though no abolitionist agitator, declared that "slavery is founded in the selfishness of man's nature—opposition to it, in his love of justice." In his first presidential campaign speech, in 1858, he said that no nation could survive half slave and half free. He was not unsympathetic to the economic plight of slaveholders, or even their constitutional property-rights arguments, but he was so identified with the abolitionist side that his very election in 1860 precipitated the secession first of South Carolina and then the other Southern states. And yet, after the Civil War had started, Lincoln declared that slavery was not really the issue; saving the Union was the issue. In fact, he held off taking any action to free the slaves in order to keep the border slave states on the Union side. "If I could save the Union without freeing any slave, I would do it," he told abolitionist gadfly Horace Greeley, not entirely ironically, in 1862. But even as he uttered these words he was planning to issue his great proclamation wherein all slaves residing in states in rebellion against the Union were declared free, as of January 1, 1863. It was, he said, a "war measure." The freed slaves, he said, "will be received into the armed services of the United States." Significantly, the Emancipation Proclamation did not free the slaves in non-rebellious states, which might have been seen as beyond even wartime constitutional limits regarding property rights.

Six months later, in July 1863, a series of battles took place over three days at Gettysburg, Pennsylvania, that proved to be the turning point of a war that by then had ranged over most of the southeastern states, from Louisiana to Virginia. The Confederates, in a push north into Maryland, nominally a Northern state, were checked at Antietam (with 23,000 dead, it was the bloodiest single day of the war for both sides). But General Robert E. Lee's later victory at Chancellorsville in northern Virginia emboldened him to make another foray north, this time up through the Valley of Virginia and into Pennsylvania.

You can revisit the awful battle that ensued at **Gettysburg National Mil-**

itary Park. They mowed each other down, the Blue and Gray, with minié balls, grapeshot, and bayonet. Children, for many of these soldiers were that young, lay screaming with their guts spilling into the summertime fields. They begged for death. Oh, you can follow the details of the battles over the three ghastly days of Gettysburg: how the two armies collided, almost by accident, west of this little farm town on the first day, July 1, which ended in defeat for the Union forces; how on the second day General Lee launched an all-out attack south of town on General Meade's federal stronghold, but was checked by federal reinforcements; how on the third day 12,000 Confederate infantrymen led by George E. Pickett attempted to break through federal lines but were repulsed—indeed slaughtered, for only one Southerner in three made it back safely behind Confederate lines. You can follow the battles closely at the park, like a real Civil War buff, making notes on maps and discussing fine points of strategy. But when you see the cemetery at Gettysburg, with its endless ranks and columns of crosses, you will remember the guts on the ground, the blood, the limbs of brothers and sons and uncles and fathers scattered among the windrows of corpses.

Lincoln was "slick," they said, when he waffled and sought compromise. On the darkest days of the war he turned everything into a joke, to the despair of his Cabinet. Even so, at the dedication of the Gettysburg National

At 4:30 A.M., on April 12, 1861, Confederate batteries began firing on Fort Sumter (now a National Monument), the last federal stronghold in Charleston Harbor, South Carolina. On Sunday, April 14, Major Robert Anderson and his 85 federal soldiers marched out of the fort and boarded a ship bound for New York. The Civil War had begun.

At Antietam National Battlefield, Maryland, this country road, known as Bloody Lane, was the site of a savage struggle during a day of battle in which more soldiers were wounded or killed than on any other single day of the Civil War. Above, Civil War battle friezes adorn monuments at Vicksburg National Military Park, Mississippi, top, and Chickamauga and Chattanooga National Military Park, Georgia/Tennessee.

A lithograph signed by Union General George C. Meade indicates military positions at the battle of Gettysburg. Fought on July 1–3, 1863, Gettysburg is seen by many historians as the military turning point of the Civil War. Although Lee's Army of Northern Virginia was able to withdraw in good order on July 4, it never again threatened the North.

Cemetery he delivered the soberest and most uncompromising political speech ever made by an American President. And he saved the Union. This brief, 267-word meditation, Lincoln's Gettysburg Address, ranks with the Declaration of Independence as a core document of the United States of America. The war had two years yet to run, and at the end of them Lincoln would lie dead of an assassin's bullet. His Gettysburg Address, however, will endure for as long as human eyes can read. Many schoolchildren have committed the words to memory. It is not a bad idea.

> Fourscore and seven years ago our fathers brought forth on this continent a new nation, conceived in liberty, and dedicated to the proposition that all men are created equal.
>
> Now we are engaged in a great civil war, testing whether that nation, or any nation so conceived and so dedicated, can long

endure. We are met on a great battlefield of that war. We have come to dedicate a portion of that field as a final resting-place for those who here gave their lives that nation might live. It is altogether fitting and proper that we should do this.

But, in a larger sense, we cannot dedicate—we cannot consecrate—we cannot hallow—this ground. The brave men, living and dead, who struggled here, have consecrated it far above our poor power to add or detract. The world will little note nor long remember what we say here, but it can never forget what they did here. It is for us, the living, rather, to be dedicated here to the unfinished work which they who fought here have thus far so nobly advanced. It is rather for us to be here dedicated to the great task remaining before us—that from these honored dead we take increased devotion to that cause for which they gave the last full measure of devotion; that

A statue of Major General Gouverneur K. Warren, above, looks out from Little Round Top, Gettysburg National Military Park. It was from this vantage point, on July 2, 1863, that Warren noted the hill's lack of defenses and promptly called in reinforcements, thus saving the day — and, perhaps, the Union.

we here highly resolve that these dead shall not have died in vain; that this nation, under God, shall have a new birth of freedom; and that government of the people, by the people, for the people, shall not perish from the earth.

When Lincoln drew his last breath, in 1865, the war had been over for less than four days. The great President was not to see the new birth of freedom. "He belongs to the ages," said his Secretary of War, Edwin Stanton.

The national park system commemorates the Civil War in many places besides Gettysburg—around two dozen places, in fact, depending on what is counted. Among them: **Appomattox Court House National Historical Park**, in Virginia, where General Lee surrendered to General Grant in a moving ceremony; **Vicksburg National Military Park**, in Mississippi, where the citizens and soldiers, cut off from supplies by Grant's forces, had to eat mule meat to stay alive; **Manassas National Battlefield Park**, in northern Virginia near a little stream named Bull Run, where the first battle after Fort Sumter was fought, with the ladies and gentlemen of Washington watching from their carriages parked at a safe distance, only to see the Union forces routed and 900 young men killed, and where a second battle was fought the following year, with 3,300 killed; **Chickamauga and Chattanooga National Military Park**, in Georgia and Tennessee, where the battle went after

On November 19, 1863 dedication day of the Gettysburg National Cemetery, President Abraham Lincoln delivered his famous Gettysburg Address, today commemorated by the Lincoln Speech Memorial, left.

Vicksburg had fallen; **Petersburg National Battlefield**, in Virginia, **Fort Donelson National Military Park**, in Tennessee; **Kennesaw Mountain National Battlefield Park**, in Georgia; **Antietam National Battlefield**, in Maryland, where so many died; **Shiloh National Military Park**, in Tennessee; **Fort Sumter**, which we have already discussed; and on through a dozen more places where we commemorate the struggle for Union.

After the war was done, three amendments were added to the Constitution—amendments to make up for the imperfection that had led to such an awful conflict. The 13th Amendment, adopted in 1865, prohibited slavery and thus extended and made constitutional Lincoln's Emancipation Proclamation. The 14th Amendment, adopted in 1868, assured the rights of citizenship to former slaves, and included the famed "due process" and "equal protection" clauses that were to form the basis of civil-rights legislation a century in the future. The 15th Amendment, adopted in 1870, specifically affirmed that "the right of citizens of the United States to vote shall not be denied or abridged by the United States or by any state on account of race, color, or previous condition of servitude." This too would figure in later struggles toward "a more perfect Union."

Thus was full citizenship given to former slaves, their equal protection under the law secured, and the specific right to vote granted. Although the amendments were, as we know, more honored in the breach, they were a beginning. Still to come, however, was the securing of such rights for women, who themselves were considered property, or the next thing to it, who did

A seven-foot-deep moat surrounds Fort Pulaski National Monument, Georgia. Until federal troops recaptured the fort on April 11, 1860, the Confederate army used it to guard the river approaches to the city of Savannah.

not possess many of the citizenship rights granted to men (including, presumably, Negro men), and who could not vote.

Though most think of "feminism"—defined here as the struggle to secure equal rights to women—as a modern political phenomenon in the United States, it does in fact predate the Civil War. Even at the time of the Constitutional Convention, women sought to secure their rights as citizens. Abigail Adams and Mercy Otis Warren pressed hard for women's rights to be included in the Constitution. But it was not until 1848 that the movement attempted an organized effort, when the first Women's Rights Convention in the United States was held at Seneca Falls, New York.

In 1848 married women had no right to property, or even to any wages they might separately earn. They had no right to divorce their husbands, who were considered to be their masters. They had no means to protect themselves under law from beatings at the hands of drunken husbands—not a small matter then or now. As for single women, the Industrial Revolution was creating a demand for inexpensive factory labor, which in many industries, especially textiles, women (along with children) were expected to provide, for 80 hours or more per week. Under the guise of "protecting" them, women were required to live in boarding houses owned by the factory proprietors, who deducted room and board from their already meager pay, perhaps two cents an hour, which was less than one-fourth the pay of men. A

Cannon, left, mark General Ulysses S. Grant's last line of defense during the battle of Shiloh, on April 6, 1862. The site is now part of Shiloh National Military Park, Tennessee.

woman, married or single, had no right to higher education or to enter the trades or professions. A woman had no right to vote and yet was taxed directly and indirectly nevertheless.

In those days prior to the Civil War—and consequently prior to the protections and prerogatives guaranteed by constitutional amendments that followed—the sentiments expressed in the Declaration of Independence and the Preamble to the Constitution had as little to do with women as they did with slaves. Accordingly, many women, sensing a common cause, became leaders in the abolitionist movement in the North as well as in the temperance movement, for there were no sure legal sanctions against wife beating by drunken husbands any more than there were sanctions against Simon Legree for beating Uncle Tom.

This, then, was the societal setting for a historical decision to issue a call for a convention to discuss the status of women in the United States. The instigator was Elizabeth Cady Stanton, born to a socially prominent family in Johnstown, New York, northwest of Albany. Athletic, enterprising, and brilliant—she excelled at Greek and debating—Stanton was a natural leader for radical causes. She married the abolitionist Henry Stanton in 1840 and settled with him in Boston, where she participated in the city's reformist intellectual circles. In 1847 the Stantons moved to Seneca Falls, New York, a small rural town in the Finger Lakes region. It was a far cry from the sophisticated American Athens that was Boston. Moreover, husband Henry was often away, leaving Elizabeth isolated and overwhelmed by housework and the care of their three children. The Stantons, like many freelance intellectuals to this day, had little money for servants.

As it happened, Elizabeth Cady Stanton complained of her plight to a circle of friends gathered for tea on a midsummer afternoon in nearby Wa-

The Clover Hill Tavern (right) and other historical buildings, above, at Appomattox Court House National Historical Park, Virginia, where General Robert E. Lee surrendered his Army of Northern Virginia to General Ulysses S. Grant on April 9, 1865. In his 1867 painting of the historic ceremony, right, artist L.M.D. Guillaume symbolized the nation's reunification by seating the two men at the same table, even though this in fact never occurred.

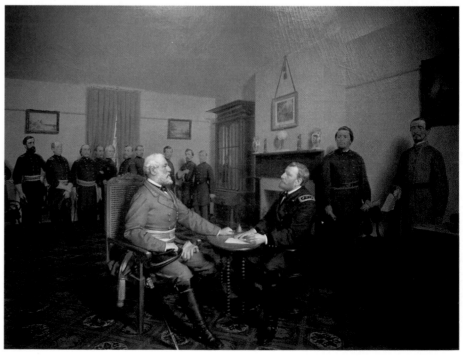

Smoke rises from the chimney of a working replica of the cabin in which Abraham Lincoln spent his youth on the Indiana frontier. The simple but sturdy cabin is on the grounds of the Lincoln Boyhood National Memorial, Lincoln City, Indiana.

terloo, New York. The discussion soon turned to the larger matters involving the status of women, and then and there the participants decided to organize what they called "the first Women's Rights Convention in the United States." Besides Stanton the organizers were Jane Hunt, Lucretia Mott, Martha Wright, and Mary Ann M'Clintock. Within a week they had drafted a document, modeled on the Declaration of Independence, entitled the Declaration of Sentiments. The difference was that this time the yoke of tyranny to be thrown off was that which men imposed on women, in contrast to the tyranny of the English king over his colonial subjects. "The history of mankind," the third paragraph of the Declaration begins, "is a history of repeated injuries and usurpations on the part of man toward woman, having in direct object the establishment of an absolute tyranny over her. To prove this, let facts be submitted to a candid world."

Among the facts submitted in the Declaration, the first was that man "has never permitted her the exercise of her inalienable right to the elective franchise." Others stated that women were, if married, "civilly dead," that they had no right to property, and that the law gave husbands "the right to deprive her of her liberty, and to administer chastisement." To the detriment of single women, the Declaration continued, if she was an owner of property, "he has taxed her to support a government which recognizes her only when her property can be made profitable to it." Also, women were denied access to "profitable employments" and, from those permitted to them, received only "scanty remuneration"; barred from teaching theology, medicine, and law; denied the facilities of a "thorough education"; excluded from the ministry; subject to a different code of "moral delinquencies" (i.e., the double standard). In short, "He has endeavored in every way that he could to destroy her confidence in her own powers, to lessen her self-respect, and to make her willing to lead a dependent and abject life." In its conclusion, the document demanded that women "have immediate admission to all the rights and privileges which belong to them as citizens of these United States."

The convention was held on July 19 and 20, 1848, at the Wesleyan Chapel in Seneca Falls. Exactly 100 women and men signed the Declaration of Sentiments, among them Frederick Douglass, the eminent abolitionist who had been born a slave.

Today some of the problems identified by the signers have been fully redressed. The right to vote, for example, was attained in 1920, though not without a great struggle, and the right to own property separate from one's husband had earlier been secured. But other rights, such as equal pay for equal work, the protection and remedies relating to wife beating, and access to the ministry, have been only partially achieved. Thus the struggle begun so unequivocally at Seneca Falls goes on. And a good way to understand it, if not participate in it, is to visit the very sites where the historic document was produced and signed—at **Women's Rights National Historical Park**. The park consists of the Elizabeth Cady Stanton House and the Wesleyan Chapel, in Seneca Falls, and, in Waterloo, the M'Clintock House, where the Declaration was drafted.

For African-Americans, the promises of the post-Civil War 13th, 14th, and 15th Amendments did not fare well. Indeed, they were intentionally withheld by Southern states after the often punitive Reconstruction-period laws were repealed or abandoned. Even the 13th Amendment, making slavery illegal, was circumvented by the sharecropping system, wherein former slaves were promised a "share" of the crop (usually cotton) that they brought in on a (white) plantation owner's land. The owners routinely cheated the sharecroppers by understating the income received from the sale of the crop; by charging outrageously high prices for seed, animals, equipment, and rent for housing; and by loaning the sharecroppers money they needed for these purposes at usurious rates. Moreover, both legal and illegal barriers were imposed to keep any blacks who might be able to afford farmland from buying it themselves—although many did despite the odds.

Beginning in the 1880s, the so-called Jim Crow laws were enacted by Southern states and municipalities to legalize racial discrimination and unequal treatment under the law, despite the 14th Amendment. The Jim Crow laws ("Jim Crow" was a character in a blackface minstrel show) made it legal to deny to all blacks equal access to public facilities, including schools, transportation, restaurants, movies, lodging, and public toilets and water fountains. Many of those reading this book can perhaps remember the "Jim Crow" railroad cars; how blacks had to go to the back doors of restaurants and eat outside, had to sit in the balconies of movie theaters, and were required to use separate toilets (or were simply barred from using them at all). "Whites Only" signs were everywhere in the South, including the border states and Washington, D.C.

In 1897 the Supreme Court, in a decision (*Plessy v. Ferguson*) that harked back to Dred Scott, affirmed that laws permitting separate facilities for blacks, including schools, were constitutional—thus establishing the doctrine of "separate but equal," with the definition of the latter term as elastic as local custom wished to make it. And the African-American population in the South was powerless to change any of it politically. Among the ploys developed to deny to the black population the franchise guaranteed by the 15th Amendment was the imposition of a poll tax, which many blacks could not afford to pay, and the requirement that those who could pay must pass a "literacy test" to determine their fitness to vote. The tests were sometimes so rigorous that not even doctors, lawyers, ministers, or college professors with doctoral degrees could pass them. Whites were not obliged to take such examinations, their "literacy" (even though they may have been illiterate) having been legislated in by "grandfather" clauses.

After World War II, the great injustice of the Jim Crow laws and the barriers to voting finally became insupportable, given the sacrifices that black soldiers had made on the battlefields of Europe and the island beaches of the South Pacific. In 1948 President Harry S Truman integrated the armed forces. In 1950 the Supreme Court required the University of Texas to admit a black student, Herman Sweatt, to its law school since no "separate but equal" institution was available for him. In 1954, in the momentous *Brown v. Board of Education* decision, the Supreme Court reversed *Plessy v. Ferguson,* stating that separate-but-equal was not equal at all and thus was unconstitutional. The late Thurgood Marshall, a lawyer for the National Association for the Advancement of Colored People (NAACP), won the case and later won a seat on the Supreme Court himself.

At the time of the *Brown v. Board of Education* decision, a 25-year-old black minister and Ph.D. candidate (the degree was awarded the next year) named Martin Luther King, Jr., was installed as pastor of the Dexter Avenue Baptist Church in Montgomery, Alabama. A year after King took this job, Rosa Parks, a 42-year-old seamstress, was arrested in Montgomery for failing to give up her seat on a city bus to a white man. And the rest, as they say, is history. The "Montgomery Improvement Association" was organized to demand reforms in transportation policy (first come first served, hire some black drivers). King was elected president of the association. The Montgomery bus boycott began. A year later, King's home was bombed. Though his young wife and their infant daughter were in the house, no one was injured.

A month after the bombing, King was arrested for conspiracy to hinder a business without "just or legal cause." But by the end of the year the Supreme Court agreed that segregation on buses was unconstitutional. By this time, Martin Luther King, Jr., was nationally famous, his picture on the cover of *Time* magazine, his meeting with President Eisenhower well publicized. Even so, he was arrested for loitering in Montgomery. He was stabbed in the chest in Harlem, but begged that his assailant, a crazed black woman, not be prosecuted. Prime Minister Nehru invited him to India to study the techniques of non-violence perfected by Mahatma Ghandi.

In 1960 King returned to the city of his birth, Atlanta, Georgia, where he founded the Southern Christian Leadership Conference and became the de facto leader of the growing civil-rights movement in America. The movement prospered, despite (or partly because of) King's being tossed in jail and hounded by the FBI, despite the beating and murder of civil-rights workers, despite a massive quasi-legal effort on the part of Southern governors and legislatures to assert states' rights in order to thwart the advances of the movement—under principles they called "interposition" and "nullification."

Then, in 1963, 200,000 people gathered on the Mall in Washington, D.C., and heard another transcendent American political speech—second only to the Gettysburg Address. "I have a dream," intoned King, his voice like a mighty chorus all by itself.

I have a dream that my four little children will one day live in a nation where they will not be judged by the color of their skin but by the content of their character…. This will be the day when all of God's children will be able to sing with new meaning, "My country 'tis of thee, sweet land of liberty, of thee I sing. Land where my fathers died, land of the pilgrim's pride, from every mountainside, let freedom ring." …[W]hen we let it ring from every village and hamlet, from every state and city, we will be able to speed up that day when all of God's children—black men and white men, Jews and Gentiles, Catholics and Protestants—will be able to join hands and to sing in the words of the old Negro spiritual, "Free at last, free at last; thank God Almighty, we are free at last."

Reforms followed. In 1964 Congress passed the Civil Rights Act; in 1965 the Voting Rights Act; and in 1968, the year that King was martyred by an assassin's bullet, the Fair Housing Act. Thus, many, though not all, of the guarantees of civil rights provided by the Constitution as amended were restored to African-Americans and other minorities. Racism could not be abolished, but at least many of the most virulent forms of governmentally instituted racism were made, finally, illegal. The era of Jim Crow was over.

What special providence made it possible for exactly the right man, Martin Luther King, Jr., to meet the needs of history so victoriously? One answer, among the many that relate to his prodigious gifts of heart and mind, is embedded in that most beautiful word *neighborhood*.

Martin Luther King, Jr., or "M.L.," as he was called in his childhood, grew up on Auburn Avenue, an older neighborhood (although nothing much is very old in Atlanta, which was burned to the ground in the Civil

The Martin Luther King, Jr., National Historic Site, in the Auburn Avenue community of Atlanta, Georgia, includes the civil-rights leader's "birth home"; the Ebenezer Baptist Church, where he preached his first sermon; and his gravesite at the Martin Luther King, Jr., Center for Nonviolent Social Change.

The Behold monument in Community Center Plaza, Martin Luther King, Jr., National Historic Site, a tribute to King's courageous efforts to forge a world in which all children can enjoy happiness, freedom, and dignity.

War) near downtown. It is today bisected by the Atlanta Freeway. There are those who argue, and with justice, that during his formative years, M.L. was undoubtedly shaped by the security and love and freedom that this middle-class neighborhood—called "Sweet Auburn"—provided him. For most of the first 12 years of his life, he lived with his mother, his father, a younger brother, an older sister, and his much-loved grandmother in an ample house at 501 Auburn Avenue. His grandfather, Adam Daniel Williams, was pastor of the Ebenezer Baptist Church, just a block and a half down the street from 501. Upon Reverend Williams's death in 1931, when M.L. was two, Martin Luther King, Sr., took over the pulpit, making the church a center for the struggle for Negro rights in Atlanta.

"The neighborhood was loaded with children," says Dean Rowley, a National Park Service historian and native Atlantan. "It was a wonderful place to grow up." The young M.L. knew the families of his neighbors—businessmen, educators, clergymen—in this close-knit community, which in effect extended the already extended family that enclosed him in a warm embrace.

The King "birth home," as it is called, and the Ebenezer Baptist Church are part of the **Martin Luther King, Jr., National Historic Site**, a two-block area along Auburn Avenue. A new visitor center is now being built that will tell the story of King's life and times. Moreover, these two blocks contain the Martin Luther King, Jr., Center for Nonviolent Social Change, founded by his widow, Coretta Scott King. The center's beautiful Freedom Hall Complex includes a museum and King's gravesite as well.

Back in the neighborhood, up the street, the house at 501 Auburn Avenue is just a house, of course—two stories, nine rooms, close to others in this urban setting. And down the street, the Ebenezer Church is just a church, with dark, creaky pews and a lighted sign outside. But there is something warm and good about these places that even (or perhaps especially) a white visitor will sense in this nurturing ground—Sweet Auburn—of the only American not a President whose day of birth is a national holiday.

One more visit and we are done with this adumbrated account of the stumbling yet often brave ways we Americans have attempted to create our "more perfect Union." We shall now discuss a unit of the national park system that is but a little patch of scruffy California desert, situated along a two-lane U.S. highway in the Owens Valley. It is **Manzanar National Historic Site**, and has a staff of one. Only one building still stands there, now used by Inyo County to house road-maintenance equipment. Two sentry posts are still intact. Otherwise only some old roads and foundations remain. A graveyard. An abandoned garden. It is a place filled with ghosts.

The story begins on December 7, 1941. Your author is 10 years old, living near Los Angeles. It is Sunday. The family has just returned home from church. Suddenly, the boy next door bursts in. "Turn on the radio! The radio!" he yells. "The Japs!" And then he dashes out again.

The Japanese had bombed Pearl Harbor. The greatest war in history, threatening for half a decade at least, had for us begun. This was a date,

THROUGH THEIR GENEROSITY THE DREAM LIVES

Toward a More Perfect Union

President Roosevelt said the following week, "that will live in infamy."

Soon the boys and girls were collecting tin cans, kitchen grease, copper tubing, newspapers, and much else for the war effort. Cars bore A or B or C gas-ration stickers. Kids lined up at the post office to buy Defense Stamps to paste in their little books to save America. But some of the kids were missing. Where were the Japanese children whose families owned the truck farms and sold produce, bright, fresh, and green, down at the market? The mothers grumbled that vegetables weren't any good anymore. In fact, many of the Orientals who lived in and around Los Angeles had simply disappeared, except for those who wore a button reading, "I am Chinese." What happened to the others? The answer was that the Japanese foreign-born as well as those so Americanized they spoke only English—old people, moms and dads, boys and girls who said "Hi" in the halls of the school and wore saddle shoes and carried blue loose-leaf notebooks on their hips and had names like Larry and Judy—all had been sent to a place called Manzanar. A prison camp. In fact, it was one of 10 American concentration camps. If the term sounds harsh, so be it. Manzanar was the first, and became the most famous. Or infamous. Seventy percent of its involuntary inmates—called "internees"—were American citizens. Once again the civil-rights amendments to the Constitution had been suspended, this time for the duration of the Second World War.

It happened because December 7 really was a day of infamy. It happened because the Imperial Army of Japan had been cruelly ravaging China and the rest of what they called, in the doublespeak of tyrannies, the "Greater East

In April 1942, San Francisco shoppers read an exclusion order directing the evacuation of people of Japanese ancestry to temporary assembly centers operated by the Wartime Civil Control Administration. A month later, photographer Dorothea Lange captured this image, opposite, of farming families boarding buses in Byron, California, bound for Turlock Assembly Center, 65 miles away.

Asia Co-Prosperity Sphere." But it also happened because of, as historian Roger Daniels has so indelicately put it, "the California racist tradition."

A part of this tradition had always been anti-Oriental. The notion of a "yellow peril" is Californian, and dates to the 1870s. Though originally associated with the "Heathen Chinee," it was, after 1886, quickly attached to the Japanese, who for the first time were permitted by their government to emigrate in significant numbers. The new Orientals that arrived in Los Angeles, San Francisco, and other Pacific Coast cities were dark-skinned, tough, smart, disciplined. Their close-knit families only proved to the paranoid Californians that the Japanese were standoffish and wanted to keep to themselves. Their very politeness was held against them as insincerity and "sneakiness." And, worst crime of all, they succeeded economically despite the legal barriers erected against them. In 1911 a federal law was enacted permitting the courts to refuse naturalization to the Japanese. In 1913 the Alien Land Bill was enacted in California to prevent the Japanese from owning land. In the 1924 Immigration Act (which figured in the Ellis Island story in Chapter 3), the immigration quota for the Japanese was zero.

Immediately after the attack on Pearl Harbor, Californians who feared that the Imperial Fleet might next strike the mainland coast descended immediately into something approaching mass hysteria concerning the Japanese. "Alert, keen-eyed citizens," editorialized the *Los Angeles Times* on December 8, should "cooperate with the military and civilian authorities

In this Dorothea Lange photograph from July 3, 1942, the American flag flutters above seemingly endless rows of barracks at Manzanar War Relocation Authority Camp, now a National Historic Site, in California's Owens Valley. Here and in similar camps, West Coast Japanese-American families were forced to endure captivity for much of World War II.

against spies, saboteurs and fifth columnists. We have thousands of Japanese here....Some, perhaps many, are...good Americans. What the rest may be we do not know, nor can we take a chance in the light of yesterday's demonstration that treachery and double-dealing are major Japanese weapons."

The military and civilian authorities quickly reached agreement that no Japanese were to be trusted. Within four weeks of Pearl Harbor, General John L. DeWitt, commander of the Western Defense Command, wired Washington that "the best people in California" wanted the Japanese removed. The best people included Senator Hiram Johnson, Governor Cuthbert L. Olsen, and state Attorney General Earl Warren. Three weeks

after that, on February 19, 1942, President Franklin Roosevelt signed Executive Order 9066, which effectively gave the War Department the authority to remove the Japanese from coastal areas. By March, a new "War Relocation Authority" was established, and the first "evacuees" arrived at Manzanar. Evacuees were given two weeks to wind up their affairs. Many could not manage it in that time and as a result lost their land and property to swindlers and corrupt officials. One strawberry farmer, about to bring in his crop, pleaded for one more week, but was denied. Before he left, he plowed the crop under—and was arrested for "destroying government property."

By August 12, 110,000 people of Japanese ancestry had been removed from the West Coast to inland camps. The population at Manzanar stood at 10,046—fishermen from Terminal Island, truck farmers from the San Fernando Valley, bobby-soxers from Fairfax High. It was, wrote Walter Rostow, "our worst wartime mistake." It constituted, said historian A. Russell Buchanan, "the most widespread disregard of personal rights since…slavery."

Manzanar was the perfect place to isolate the Japanese. The arid Owens Valley of eastern California is enclosed between the great wall of the Sierras to the west and the Inyo and White mountains to the east. The camp was built on land owned by the Los Angeles Department of Power and Water. (For the grotesque story, loosely told, of how L.A. euchred this valley 200 miles to the north of the city out of its precious water, see the film "Chinatown"—the one in which Jack Nicholson gets his nostril slit.) The land, which earlier had been abandoned by orchardists (Manzanar means "apple orchard" in Spanish), was flat and dry, and nearly waterless, thanks to Los Angeles. Flimsy wood-and-tar-paper barracks had been built by the Army to house this new population, instantly creating the largest city between Reno and Los Angeles. The barracks were sited side by side in endless ranks and files as far as the eye could see in the 550-acre compound. Each 20-by-100-foot structure was divided into four or five partitioned spaces, of between 360 and 480 square feet. Each "apartment," as camp officials described them, housed a family of up to seven people. The partitions did not reach to the ceiling. There was no indoor plumbing. The internees ate in mess halls and were required to use latrines with no provision for privacy. The old people, the Issei, born in Japan, for whom personal privacy and dignity were essential parts of their tradition and character, waited until midnight. Some committed ritual suicide. Some just wasted away. Some fell into alcoholism. Their shame—though they had no idea what they had done—was too much to bear.

And yet, despite this bizarre injustice, somehow these Americans not only survived, they triumphed. The erstwhile truck farmers started a new farm and grew the beautiful vegetables no longer enjoyed by the matrons of Los Angeles. They created schools in which Catholic nuns and Quakers trained a new generation, the Nisei, who went on to become leaders in industry, science, higher education, and law in postwar America. And they made beautiful gardens. "Near Block 28," writes Jeanne Wakasuki Houston in her charming memoir, *Farewell to Manzanar*, "some of the men who had been professional gardeners built a small park, with mossy nooks, ponds, waterfalls and curved wooden bridges." And each barracks had its own garden.

"People who lived in Owens Valley during the war still remember the flowers and lush greenery they could see from the highway as they drove past the main gate."

And finally, they became the greatest of patriots during the war. The all-Nisei 100th Battalion of the 442nd Regimental Combat Team, whose soldiers were drawn from Hawaii and the mainland camps, was the most decorated American unit for its size in World War II and suffered one of the highest levels of casualties. In the barracks windows of Manzanar hung the Blue Star flags just like every place else in America, signifying a family member at arms overseas, but with more of them turning to Gold, when a beloved son or brother or father was killed. Other unsung heroes were some 6,000 soldiers of the Military Intelligence Service—a group of Japanese-Americans whose exploits rival any in World War II history, but which remain largely unknown due to oaths of secrecy taken before their discharge.

It is a complicated story, and one with great internal struggle within the community at Manzanar: a riot in which two were killed and 11 injured; charges of *uni*—disloyalty within the Japanese community—leveled against those who cooperated too closely with authorities, especially in the early years; and, yes, deep resentment, especially over the requirement that the internees sign a loyalty oath. "No self-respecting espionage agent," writes Jeanne Wakasuki Houston, "would willingly admit he was disloyal. Yet the very idea of the oath itself—appearing at the end of that first chaotic year—became the final goad that prodded many once-loyal citizens to turn militantly anti-American." Still, there was not a "single case of Japanese disloyalty or sabotage during the whole war," wrote historian Henry Steele Commager on the basis of FBI information.

To understand the meaning of Manzanar, one might well begin at the Eastern California Museum, in Independence, California, which has an exhibit, constantly being updated, on life at Manzanar, created primarily by those who were interned there. The museum director, Bill Michael, tells how some people in the Owens Valley, especially war veterans not so willing to forget their suffering at the hands of the Japanese, have vigorously objected to the memorialization of Manzanar. Some have berated Michael soundly for his sympathetic presentation of the Manzanar story. But not all. One day, a burly man in his 60s who was visiting the museum approached Michael, who feared he was in for another complaint. The visitor said he was a farmer from Fresno, and explained to Michael how during the 1940s his Japanese friends at school had just disappeared. "He told me," says Michael, "that he didn't really understand what had happened until he had visited our museum and been out to Manzanar. And as he was telling me this, the tears just started flowing down his face."

Ross Hopkins, a supervisory National Park Service ranger, is the putative superintendent at Manzanar. He has been working on plans for the place since it was authorized as a historic site in 1992. But no on-site development has yet begun, since no operating budget was established by the National Park Service until 1994. Hopkins hopes the park service can one day reconstruct one or two of the barracks at Manzanar, and perhaps some of the gardens. He is energized by the idea of explaining to visitors who were born

Young soldiers in the all-Nisei (Japanese-American) 100th Battalion of the 442nd Regimental Combat Team, one of the most decorated American units in World War II.

after World War II just how it was. Ironically, his own father was an Army Air Corps fighter pilot killed in World War II, so his historic sympathy for the people of Manzanar is not counterfeit and carries a special resonance. Hopkins wants to install markers showing where all the barracks stood before they were torn down at the end of the war. That way, says Hopkins, the people interned here, who will never forget their Manzanar block and barracks numbers, can find them for themselves and can pass them along to their descendants. He also wants to support oral-history projects so that life at Manzanar can be understood and interpreted down to its most intimate details. There is not much time left to do this, he realizes, for now only a few of the first-generation Issei are still alive, and their children, the Nisei, are growing older.

Several years ago the U.S. Congress enacted legislation that would pay reparations to interned Japanese-Americans. The money is welcome, of course, but, as Hopkins says, they attach as much importance to the official apology offered by the President of the United States. That it was George Bush, himself shot down by the Japanese in the Pacific Theater, makes the gesture all the more meaningful.

Manzanar is a unit of the national park system that memorializes not some triumph of our history, but a mistake. A terrible mistake. That this internment camp could be a national park says more about the decency of this uniquely American enterprise, the national park system, than even the most exalted landscape or battlefield. Manzanar was a thoroughgoing American community that today provides a crash course in patriotism. And, despite its lack of budget and staff, it is a park not to be missed. The ghosts here include, after all, the better angels of our nature.

STUDY OUT
THE LAND

This land is your land,
This land is my land
From California
To the New York island.
From the redwood forest
To the Gulf Stream waters,
This land was made for you and me.

—Woody Guthrie
American Folk Song

If American history teaches us anything, it is that we are one nation, indivisible. We are not to be torn asunder by section or faction or by race, national origin, or gender. Therefore, white people must visit Sweet Auburn, and sit in the pews of the Ebenezer Baptist Church, and tour the home of Martin Luther King, Jr. Black people must visit Seneca Falls, where Frederick Douglass signed the Declaration of Sentiments. Native Americans should visit the Jefferson Memorial. Lutheran farmers from the Upper Midwest should visit the place where Father Kino ministered to the Pimas in Arizona. The grandchildren of those who arrived, terrified and jubilant, at Ellis Island should tour the ruins at Chaco. And everyone, of course, must visit the Grand Canyon, where the layers of rock tell our geological story; the Everglades, where nature's delicate balances are revealed; Yosemite Valley, where lies the most beautiful mountain scenery on Earth; and the other crown jewels of our park system.

These are journeys into our natural and cultural history—geological, anthropological, sociological, ecological, political—that this book has proposed and that our system of national parks makes available to us. But there are more possibilities than we have even hinted at. Indeed, we have dealt only sketchily with the categories we selected, and we have not dealt at all, for example, with the history of our technology that is expressed by the **Wright Brothers National Memorial** at Kitty Hawk on the outer banks of North Carolina, or the **Edison National Historic Site** in East Orange, New Jersey. We have not discussed units of the system celebrating the nation's literary and artistic achievements—the **Longfellow National Historic Site** in

Sunset over Johnson's Landing on the St. Croix River, which, together with the Namekagon River, constitutes the 252-mile St. Croix National Scenic Riverway, in Minnesota and Wisconsin.

Cambridge, Massachusetts, or the **Weir Farm National Historic Site** in Ridgefield, Connecticut, where J. Alden Weir, the American impressionist painter, had his studio. We did not mention the sites associated with American Presidents—the homes, memorials, monuments, and museums of Lincoln, Adams, Andrew Johnson, Lyndon Johnson, Eisenhower, Grant, Washington, Truman, Hoover, Theodore Roosevelt, Franklin Delano Roosevelt, Garfield, Carter, Kennedy, Van Buren, Jefferson, Grant, Taft. Our list of omissions is lengthy and chastening.

Therefore, those who wish to study out the land (in Thomas King Whipple's phrase)—to take the measure of their country with care, precision, and intentionality—should first consider which basic categories interest them and then choose the individual park units they may wish to visit. What is most important in the planning is that there *be* one—a plan. A haphazard visit to a national park is like a haphazard visit to a public library. Impressive, possibly, but not really edifying. Contained within the parks, just as in the libraries, is the true pleasure of *knowledge*. But it cannot be apprehended by

Clockwise from right: "the Parachute," a cave formation in Lehman Caves, Great Basin National Park, Nevada; lava formations on the Kipahulu coast (Maui), Haleakala National Park, Hawaii; Grinnell Lake, Glacier National Park, Montana; and sandstone boulders before El Capitan, Guadalupe Mountains National Park, Texas.

A long succession of alternating frosts and thaws eroded Delicate Arch, in Utah's Arches National Park, from an isolated sandstone wall. At left, the stem of a soaptree yucca, such as this one in White Sands National Monument, New Mexico, can grow up to a foot a year to keep the plant's leaves above the shifting sands.

a quick park-road drive-through any more than it can be communicated through the spines of the volumes on a library's shelves.

Now let us suppose you are convinced by this little diatribe that, yes, you will do some planning. How does one go about it? The answer is to get hold of at least one, or possibly all three, of the books that briefly describe *all* the units of the national park system. They are the following:

• *The Complete Guide to America's National Parks*, published by the National Parks Foundation and distributed by Fodors/Random House. It is available from most bookstores. If a store does not have it on hand, ask the clerk to order it for you. The *Guide*, 540 pages, costs about $15 (paperback), and is updated every two years. It contains a brief description of parks units (listed by state), how to get there, chief features, camping and lodging information, and much else.

• *The National Parks: Index 1993* (the most recent edition at this writing), published by the Office of Public Affairs of the National Park Service and distributed by the Superintendent of Documents, U.S. Government Printing Office, Washington, D.C. 20420. This handy booklet lists all the units in the system by state, and provides for each a brief description plus the address and phone number of the park headquarters.

• *The National Parks*, by Freeman Tilden, edited and updated by Paul Schullery, published by Knopf. This book, first issued in 1951 and last revised by Schullery in 1986, is currently out of print. One hopes the publisher is at work on a new edition, but an old one may be found at some bookshops for about $17, paperback. This is a delightful compendium, with brief essays on each unit of the system by the "father" of national park interpretation—the art of making parks come alive to their visitors through ranger-led walks, campfire talks, exhibits, films, and publications. The book is not a directory, but those lucky enough to find a copy should not let it out of their sight. It is a treasure.

After a look through the listings in the books noted above, your purposeful discover-America planning can begin. Let us say you have now chosen one or more categories of parks that interest you. And that you have se-

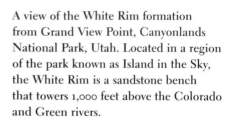

A view of the White Rim formation from Grand View Point, Canyonlands National Park, Utah. Located in a region of the park known as Island in the Sky, the White Rim is a sandstone bench that towers 1,000 feet above the Colorado and Green rivers.

lected some of the park system units you wish to visit. What next? The answer is: read first, then visit. Unfortunately, the opposite is usually the case. We decide to visit a park. We use a road map to get there. We receive a brochure at the entry gate. We wander around. We buy some pamphlets at the park bookstore. We go home. Then we read about all the features we didn't know to look for when we were there.

The trick is to turn that order of events upside down. Do this: Write to the park superintendent, whose address is given on the back of the map accompanying this book, and ask for some background material. State in your letter what your particular interest may be. The superintendent, or another staff member, will send you the park's basic brochure and map plus materials of many kinds. You might well ask specifically for a brief bibliography of published materials if you have time for detailed study before your visit. In any case, try this just once. You will be amazed at how responsive park officials can be, and how much better your visit will turn out.

Now, let us say you and the family have arrived at the park. You are reasonably familiar with what to look for. Therefore, you set out on your own to see for yourself. Wrong. The park service prides itself on interpretation and will go to extraordinary lengths to make sure that any visitor willing to take the ranger-guided walks or attend the campfire lectures will learn something to enrich his or her experience that no book or brochure can ever impart. It may seem corny to some to sign up for these activities, but that's the stratagem you must use. Be corny! And do it at the beginning of your visit. Then, with new understandings in hand, you can deepen the experience by striking out on your own.

A final word. At many if not most of the park units you visit you will notice that some of the exhibits are old, that there are too few staff for inter-

Rainfall at Mesquite Flat dunes, left, in Death Valley National Monument, California, averages less than two inches per year. Below, petrified logs in the Blue Mesa region of Petrified Forest National Park, Arizona, date back some 220 million years.

pretation, that the heavily used areas of the parks are not maintained as well as they might be. You should know that these deficiencies are entirely a reflection of the amount of money Congress appropriates to the operation of the park system. They have nothing to do with the skill or commitment of park personnel. You will have difficulty finding anyone in the United States government, in any branch, who does not express admiration for the dedication, knowledge, and energy of the people who serve us in our national parks. They are nearly as much a national treasure as the parks themselves.

But the parks have now fallen, once again, on hard times. Some of the damage due to low budgets cannot be undone, but much of it can. The museum at Homestead National Monument, for example, can and should be improved. Much more archaeological and anthropological research is needed at Hopewell Culture, the Grand Canyon trails need to be kept up better, means to cope with the hordes of visitors at Yosemite should be developed, Manzanar needs trained Japanese-American rangers and the money to recreate some of the features of the camp. Volunteers are welcome at all the parks, and perhaps some of those reading this book will wish to offer their ser-

The National Park Service's seashores include Point Reyes, top, just north of San Francisco; Second Beach, top right, in Olympic National Park, Washington; the dunes of Cumberland Island National Seashore, Georgia, above right; Crescent Beach, below right, in Redwood National Park, California; and Race Point, below left, along Cape Cod National Seashore, Massachusetts.

vices. For example, the Sierra Club organizes several volunteer maintenance outings every year to help out at Chaco Culture National Historical Park.

At the same time, Congress must take responsibility, too. At this writing—and we expect the trend to continue—Congress is bent on reducing the national park system budget. In this regard, it is well to remember that legislators can change their minds. Congress has denied funds in the past to the parks, only to restore them later. Wrote Bernard DeVoto in 1954, "The progressive impairment of the parks by budgetary bloodletting is a national disgrace." He was right then, and the words apply today as well.

Thus, visitors to the parks who see the defects should not be disappointed but take them as a challenge and a spur to action—to do one's part by being a good park visitor oneself, to volunteer to work in park programs, and to urge lawmakers to mend their ways. Our parks are, after all, the very core of the American experience, not some minor governmental function. If we are to discover America, there must be some of it left to discover. And so our journeys to the parks have a dual role—to educate and entertain us, and to move us to ensure that future generations will have that privilege, too.

Withal, this is how we propose that you study out the land. Who knows? Perhaps you will find *America* there.

Have a good trip!

Northwestern Fjord, Kenai Fjords National Park, Alaska. The steep-sided fjords, carved by glaciers, were created as the seaward ends of the Kenai Mountains were dragged into the Gulf of Alaska by the collision of two of the Earth's tectonic plates.

ACKNOWLEDGMENTS

In a very real sense, this book is not only a collaboration between writer, photographer, and consultant (i.e., the undersigned), but of the three of us with a large number of park officials, scientists, and historians who worked with us on the project, and with the editors at Smithsonian Books who have brought this volume into being.

To begin with, we are indebted to a panel of nationally known authorities on the parks and the history surrounding them for advice in selecting the park units featured in this book. The panel included William C. Everhart, John Hope Franklin, Michael Frome, M. J. Gladstone, Jesse Jennings, Michael Kammen, John G. Mitchell, Paul N. Perrot, Harold Pinkett, Marian Albright Schenck, and Robin W. Winks.

In addition, we are obliged to Barry Mackintosh, Bureau Historian, National Park Service, for assistance throughout the project; to Tom Durant, Tereza Vazquez de Vado, and Nancy McLoughlin at the park service's Harpers Ferry Center for providing many of the historical images used in the book; to anthropologist David J. Meltzer, of Southern Methodist University, and to historian, author, and publisher Arthur M. Lee for reviewing sections of the manuscript; to William C. Duddelson, Nancy Shute, and Darlene Thomas for supplying useful background information; and to Roger G. Kennedy, current Director of the National Park Service, for his generous support of our work.

As the parks themselves (and in some cases associated institutions), we were given a gracious reception and an impressive amount of information and material assistance in our photographic and research visits (not to mention telephone interviews, correspondence, and park-specific manuscript review) by park service staff. We do not have enough space for assignments, titles, honorifics, and names, too. And so, here are the names, offered with sincere thanks: Bruce Anderson, Larry N. Beane, Shirley Beccue, Lawrence A. Belli, Robert Burgoon, Dan Chure, Rick Cook, Chuck Dale, Constantine J. Dillon, Gary W. Easton, Ann Elder, Robert A. Fliegel, Dabney Ford, Don Garate, Dennis Hamm, Lance Hatten, Ross R. Hopkins, Robert Hyder, Andrew A. Kling, Becky Lacome, Mardie Lane, Scott Madsen, Bill Michael, Bob Moore, Barry Moreno, Jon Newman, Chris Niewold, Robert Peterson, Pat Phelan, Greer Price, Ellis Richard, Dean Rowley, Vivien Ellen Rose, Farrell Saunders, Alan J. Smigielski, Brian Suderman, David Whitman, C. T. Wilson, Gordon J. Wilson, and Joseph W. Zarki. To those whose names we have inadvertently omitted from this list, our deepest apologies.

Finally, we are indebted to the staff of Smithsonian Books—Alex Doster, Amy Donovan, Frances Rowsell, and others—for their professionalism and remarkable skill in making beautiful, telling books; and to Ila Little, Bonnie Meunch, and Ann Rath, who shared our travels, provided crucial creative assistance, helped keep the project on track, and otherwise made the whole business possible.

We are grateful to you, one and all.

Charles E. Little
David Muench
Frederick L. Rath, Jr.

PICTURE CREDITS

ACKNOWLEDGEMENTS

Tom DuRant, Curator, and Teresa Vazquez de Vado, Technical Information Specialist, National Park Service, Historic Photographic Collections, Harpers Ferry Center, Virginia; Nancy Mc Loughlin, Trade Specialist, NPS, Division of Publications, Harpers Ferry Center, Virginia; Judy Goldin, Research; Bonnie Muench, Stefanie Muench, and Zandria Muench Beraldo, David Muench's staff; Tom Suzuki Design, Inc.

Mission San José. *See* San Antonio Missions NHP.
Missionaries: Franciscans, 103, 107, **111**, 112; Jesuits or "Black Robes," 103, 108, 111, 112, 148
Mississippi River, 7, 162, **182, 185**
Missouri Compromise, 185
Montgomery Improvement Association, Alabama, 199
Monticello, Virginia, 181
Monuments: Civil War, **188–189**; National, **192–193**
Moran, Thomas: *Grand Canyon of the Yellowstone* (painting), **17**
Morison, Samuel Eliot, 178
Mott, Lucretia, 197
Mount Desert Island, Maine, 148, 152
Mount Katahdin, Maine, **166**
Mount McKinley. *See* Denali NP.
Mount Rainier National Park, Washington, 21, **35**, 37, 148; Tatoosh Range, 35
Muench, David, 7, 9
Muir, John, **21**, 24, 146–148
Museum of Westward Expansion, Missouri, 183

Narváez, Pánfilo de, 107
Natchez Trace Parkway, Alabama/Mississippi/Tennessee, 10
National Audubon Society, 169, 170
National Capital Parks, 33
National Geographic Society, 83, 86
National Park Service, 7, 8, 20, 24, **27**, 30, 32, 33, 35, 49–50, 81, 86, 105, 162, 164, 181, 185, 202, 208; directors, 8; establishment of, 148; headgear, 20, interpretive program, **147**; public affairs, 213. *See also* individual parks.
National Parks: Index 1993 (book), 213
Native Americans, 77; Aleut, 78; Algonquian, 115; Amerind, 78; Apache, 78; Athabaskan, 78, **78**, 92; Aztec, 90, 96, Chacoan, 92; Chickasaw, 10; Delaware, 87; Havasupai, 56; Mandan, 181; Miami, 87; Navaho, 78, 92; Paleo Indian, 78; Pima, 108, **108**, 211; Shawnee, 87, 91; Shoshone, 181; Toltecs, 91; Zuni, 107
Navajo National Monument, Arizona, **98**, **101**; Keet Seel ruins, **98**
Negro slavery, 121
Nelson, Edward W., 77
New England, 15, 161, 164
New Galicia, 107, 111, 112
New World, **74**, 78, 115, **117**; Europeans arriving in, 102; Spanish empire in, 103
New York City, 95, 121, 152; Battery Park, 135; Manhattan, **131**, 133; North River, 130
New York State Historical Association, 9
Nisei, 207; units in World War II, **209**. *See also* Japanese-Americans.
Niza, Marcos de, 107
Nogales, 108
Nordic explorers, 78
Norse people, 102
Northwest Territories, 181
Notes on Virginia (book), 180
Nunivak Island, Alaska, **75**

Ohio, 90; Marietta, 88; Chillecothe, 90
Ohio and Mississippi River drainages, 91
Old Courthouse, (St. Louis) Missouri, 185
Old North Church. *See* Boston NHP.
Old World, **74**, 78, 115, 137

Olsen, Govenor Cuthbert L., 206
Olympic National Park, Washington, 148, **155**; Hoh Rain Forest, **155**; Olympic Peninsula, **155**; Second Beach, **216**; Taylor Point, **155**
Ordinance of 1787 or Northwest Ordinance, 181
Outer Banks, North Carolina, 115, **117**, 118, 120, 211
Owens Valley, California, 202

Pacific Ocean, 46, 76, **155, 182**
Paine, Thomas: *Common Sense* (pamphlet), 176
Parks, Rosa, 199
Pea Island National Wildlife Refuge, North Carolina, 117
Peale, A. C., **23**
Pearl Harbor, Hawaii, 202, 205
Pecos Indians, 102
Pecos National Historical Park, New Mexico, 102
Pele, goddess, 44–45, 47
Petersburg National Battlefield, Virginia, 193
Peterson, O. A., 63
Peterson, Robert, 91
Petrified Forest National Park, Arizona, **215**; Blue Mesa, **215**
Pettinga, Barbara, 143
Philadelphia Philosophical Society, 181
Phoenicians, 91
Pickett, General George E., 187
Pilgrims, landing in Massachusetts, 120
Pimería Alta region, 108, 111
Plants: angiosperm, 165; bald cypress, 169; basswoods, 165; beech, 164; birch, 164; buckeye, 165; deciduous forest, 164; dwarf cypress, **168**; evergreen hemlock, 164; fir, 164; gumbo limbo, 169; hickory, 165; magnolia, 165; mangrove, 169; maple, 165; mesophytic woodlands, 164; oak, 164–165, 169; Ohia-hapuu tree fern, 48; lysiloma, 169; pine, 164, 169; royal palm, 169; saw grass, 168, **168, 169**; slash pine, 169; soaptree yucca, 213; sprucc, 164; sweetgum, 165; tulip poplar, 165
Plate tectonics, 41–43, **42**, 46; asthenosphere, 41, 47; continental drift, 42; crust, 42, 47; Eurasian plate, 46; Gondwanaland, 41; Gulf of Alaska, 217; Laurasia, 41; lithosphere, 41, 42, 47; mantle, 47; Mohole project, 47–48; Mohorovičić discontinuity, 47–48; North American plate, 41, 42, 46, 51; Pacific plate, 42, 45, 51; Pangea, 41, 42; rift zone, 44; Tethys Sea, 41
Plessy vs Ferguson, 199
Pocahontas, **120**
Point Reyes National Seashore, California, **216**
Polar North, 81
Powell, John Wesley, 48–49, **51**
Powhatan, **120**
Pre-Columbian civilization, 87
Presidents: Adams, John, 212; Bush, George, 81, 209; Carter, Jimmy, 37, 212; Clinton, William, 17; Eisenhower, Dwight, 199, 212; Garfield, James, 212; Grant, Ulysses S., 212; Hoover, Herbert, 30, 212; Jefferson, Thomas, 16, 91, 111, 121, 137, 177, 180, 181, 212; Johnson, Andrew, 212; Johnson, Lyndon, 37, 135, 212; Kennedy, John, F., 86, 212; Lincoln, Abraham, 17, 121, 186, 187, 192, **193, 197**, 212; Madison, James, 121, 180; Nixon, Richard, 37; Roosevelt, Franklin

Delano, 8, 30, 32, 212; Roosevelt, Theodore, **21**, 22, 23, 146, **150**, 170, 212; Taft, William H., 212; Truman, Harry S, 168, 199, 212; Van Buren, Martin, 212; Washington, George, 181, 212; Wilson, Woodrow, **27**, 162
Pueblo Bonito. *See* Chaco Culture NHP.
Pueblos: Pecos, 102; Taos, 102

Queen Elizabeth I, 115, 118

Raleigh, Sir Walter, **114**, 113–118; 1584 expedition, 117
Red Rock Lakes, Montana, 142
Redwood National Park, California, 37, **216**; Crescent Beach, **216**
Revere, Paul, 176
Revolution: American, 118; Industrial, 125
Rickover, Hyman, 135
Ridley, Oscar, 86
Roanoke Island, North Carolina, **114**, 115, 118; fort at, 120; lost colony, 120
Rockefeller, John D., 162
Rockne, Knute, 135
Rocky Mountains or Rockies, 51, 87, 121, 182, **182**; northern, 91
Roosevelt, Eleanor, 32
Rostow, Walter, 207
Rowley, Dean, 202
Runte, Alfred, 16, 21, 27, 162
Russell Cave National Monument, Alabama, 82–83, 85, **85**, 86; "Indian Days" celebration, 87
Russia, 81

Saarinen, Eero, 183
Sacajawea, 181
Salinas Pueblo Missions National Monument, New Mexico, 73, 101; Salinas district, 73; San Gregorio de Abò church, **73**
San Antonio Missions National Historical Park, Texas, **111**; Mission San José, **111**
San Francisco Bay, California, **135**
San Gregorio de Abò church. *See* Salinas Pueblo Missions NM.
San Juan River basin, 92, 98–101
Sandburg, Carl: "Cornhuskers" (poem) 73
Santa Fe trail at Great Bend, Kansas, **122**
Saugus Iron Works National Historic Site, Massachusetts, 37
Saunders, Farrell, 83, 87
Scandinavia, 91, 122
Schulery, Paul, 213
Scioto River, 87; Scioto-Ohio River valley region, 91
Scott, Dred, 185, 199
Scribners Monthly (magazine), **24**
Seneca Falls, New York, 194, 195, 198, 211; Wesleyan Chapel in, 198; Women's Rights Convention at, 194
Sequoia National Park, California, 21, 148, **155**; General Sherman tree, **155**; Giant Forest grove, 32; Sierra Nevada, **33**, 148
Serra, Father Junipero, 108
Seven Cities of Cibola, 107
Seward Peninsula, 81; Cape Prince of Wales, 81
Shaw, George Bernard, 10
Shay's Rebellion, 177

Discover America was designed by Tom Suzuki, Tom Suzuki, Inc., Falls Church, VA, assisted by Hae-Ran Cho, Constance D. Dillman, and Shaya Kraut. Digital-type composition and page layout were originated on an Apple Macintosh Power PC 8100 utilizing Quark XPress and Adobe Illustrator. The text type is 11pt Electra LH with 9pt Electra LH Bold captions. Color separation and film output were provided by Colotone Imaging, Branford, CT. Four-color web printing and binding were done at Rand McNally, Versailles, KY, on 70# Somerset Gloss. The endsheets are Ecological Fibers 80# Rainbow Antique and the book cloth is Holliston Kingston.

DISCOVER AMERICA